Productivity Kit

Adobe Press

San Jose, California

Productivity Kit

Adobe Press
San Jose, California

Library of Congress Catalog No.: 98-85101

ISBN: 1-56830-464-1

10 9 8 7 6 5 4 3 2 First Printing: January 1999

Published by Adobe Press, Adobe Systems Incorporated, San Jose, California.

Adobe Press books are published and distributed by Macmillan Computer Publishing USA. For information on Adobe Press books address Macmillan Computer Publishing USA, 201 West 103rd Street, Indianapolis, Indiana, 46290 or visit Macmillan's World Wide Web page (http://www.mcp.com/hayden/adobe).

Part Number: 90014878

Contents

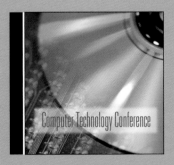

Introduction

The *Adobe Photoshop Productivity Kit* provides ideas, techniques, templates, and automated actions to help you get the most out of Adobe® Photoshop® image-editing software and Adobe ImageReady™ software for optimizing Web graphics.

Using your photographs, logos, and artwork, you can produce professional-looking materials for your business or organization—and learn practical techniques that you can apply to other projects. The accompanying CD-ROM supplies dozens of ready-made actions and templates (including Adobe PageMaker® page layouts) that you can use to produce your materials easily and efficiently.

Using tryout software and other Adobe products

Many of the projects contain templates and tips for use with Adobe products such as PageMaker or ImageReady. If you do not own these products, you can use the tryout versions supplied on the CD-ROM. These tryout versions of software provide limited functionality and expire 30 days after installation.

The ready-made templates use only basic fonts available on most computers, but you can enhance your projects by choosing other fonts. Visit the Adobe Web site, www.adobe.com, for information on purchasing fonts

shown in this book. (A complete list of these fonts appears at the back of this book.) The Adobe Web site also provides information on purchasing full versions of Adobe software.

Using the projects

This book contains step-by-step instructions and design tips for a variety of projects—from touching up photographs to creating newsletters, slides, postcards, posters, CD covers, ads, and animated Web page banners. Many projects include variations and a choice of templates to help you customize your work.

To get started, follow the instructions in "Getting Your Photos Ready for Projects" to trim, size, and color-correct your source photo. Then proceed to any project to create the materials of your choice. Because each project provides stand-alone instructions, there's no need to complete the projects in the order that they appear in the book. Just pick the project suited to your needs, and prepare to get productive!

Tools:

Adobe Photoshop

Materials:

Your photo

Getting Your Photos Ready for Projects

Start here to set up, trim, and color-correct your photo before beginning a project.

Use the instructions in this chapter to prepare your photo and set up Adobe Photoshop for use in the Productivity Kit projects. This chapter will help you fix many of the common alignment, size, and tonal problems that can result from scanning or capturing a photo file. Although you can perform limited color corrections in Adobe ImageReady, Photoshop offers the full range of color-correction tools.

Before editing your photo or beginning a project, review the following recommendations. This preliminary checklist will help to ensure smooth project workflow:

Work with a copy of your photo.
It's good practice to work with a copy of your original photo file. This way, you can preserve your original photo for re-editing or use in other projects.

Work in 8 Bits/Channel mode.
If you've opened a photo taken with a digital camera, the photo file may be set to 16 Bits/Channel. This setting increases the amount of color information in the photo but also makes many Photoshop commands temporarily unavailable. To ensure full use of Photoshop commands, choose Image > Mode > 8 Bits/Channel.

Work in RGB mode. Unless otherwise noted, most of the projects require that your starting photo be set to RGB mode. Choose Image > Mode > RGB Color to set your photo to this mode. Although projects include converting your photo to CMYK mode

as a final step for high-end printing, most of the editing in these projects is performed in RGB mode.

Restore default preferences.
Photoshop stores many of its program settings, such as the default values in dialog boxes, in a Preferences file. If you want to ensure that tools and palettes function as described in the Productivity Kit, quit Photoshop and delete the Adobe Photoshop 5.0 Prefs file (or rename the file if you want to keep your custom program settings). The Prefs file is usually located in the Photoshop\Photoshop Settings folder.

To restore default preferences for ImageReady, quit the application and do one of the following:

• In Windows, use the Registry Editor to restore ImageReady preferences to their default settings. See the online documentation accompanying Registry Editor for information.

• In Mac® OS, open the Preferences folder in the System Folder and rename the Adobe ImageReady 1.0 Prefs file, or drag the file to the Trash.

Once you've specified preliminary settings, you're ready to straighten, resize, and color-correct your photo. Since each photo has its own set of problems, you need perform only those corrections that apply to your photo.

Scan the photo at the correct size

Many of the projects recommend specific dimensions and resolution values for the starting photo. If you're planning to use a scanned file, try to scan the photo as close to the recommended values as possible; you can always fine-tune the photo's measurements by using the "Crop and refine the photo size" steps later in this chapter. If you're planning to crop your photo significantly, scan at a resolution higher than the recommended value.

A basic understanding of digital image concepts will help you scan and size your photos effectively.

Pixels. The digital images that you work with in Photoshop and ImageReady are composed of small data squares called pixels. Each pixel is assigned a specific location and color value in the image; together, the pixels make up the appearance of the image. The total number of pixels in an image determines the image's file size, usually measured in kilobytes (K) or megabytes (MB).

Resolution. Resolution is the number of pixels contained per unit of printed length in an image, usually measured in pixels per inch (ppi). You can usually specify a resolution as you scan an image; you can also change the resolution when working in Photoshop. In general, a higher resolution translates to better, more detailed print quality. For images that will appear exclusively online, you needn't bother with high resolutions; 72 pixels/inch, the resolution displayed by many computer monitors, is sufficient for online images.

Note the change in file size, pixel count, and resolution in the images below. The net effect of more pixels in the same print dimensions is better print quality but also greater file size.

16K file size
72 x 108 pixel dim.
1" x 1.5" print size
72 ppi resolution

176K file size
200 x 300 pixel dim.
1" x 1.5" print size
200 ppi resolution

The following is a guide to the resolution ranges appropriate to different outputs:

72 ppi—For screen viewing of Web pages or online materials.

120–150 ppi—For output to typical desktop laser and ink-jet printers.

200–250 ppi—For most professional offset presses and direct printing of items such as color magazines or brochures.

Resampling. When you adjust the dimensions or resolution of an image, Photoshop sometimes increases (resamples up) or decreases (downsamples) the pixel count and file size to match the target measurements. In general, you should try to downsample your images rather than resample up. Resampling up can degrade your image quality, as Photoshop adds new pixels by estimating their approximate color values.

For example, it's safe to decrease the resolution of an image (and therefore downsample it) for online use. However, the reverse is not true. Increasing the resolution of an image (for uses such as offset printing) will usually degrade the image quality. Instead, you should rescan or capture the original image at a higher resolution to avoid resampling up.

72 ppi image resampled up to 150 ppi results in poor image quality

300 ppi image downsampled to 150 ppi results in adequate image quality

Crop and refine the photo size

When you open a scanned photo in Photoshop, you may notice some basic problems such as misalignment or ragged edges. Or you may want to resize a scanned or stock photo for a project or use just a portion of the photo.

Trim and resize the photo. Select the crop tool (✠) and select Fixed Target Size in the Options palette. Enter the Width and Height values recommended by the project (use the pop-up menus to change the units of measure), and leave the Resolution text box empty.

Drag in the photo to draw a bounding box around the area you want to keep.

• To reposition the bounding box, drag inside the bounding box.

• To adjust the size of the bounding box, drag a handle on the box.

• To rotate the bounding box, position the pointer outside the bounding box (the pointer turns into a curved arrow) and drag.

To crop the photo, press Enter. To cancel the cropping operation, press Esc.

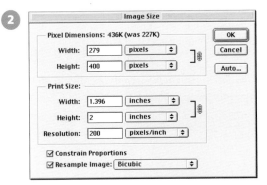

Check the photo resolution. Choose Image > Image Size, select Resample Image. Note the Resolution value listed:

• If the value is lower than the project's recommended resolution, click Cancel and rescan the photo at a higher resolution. Increasing your photo's resolution using the Image Size command would result in resampling up to a higher file size (see "Resampling" on page 5).

• If the value is higher than the project's recommended resolution, enter the recommended value for Resolution and click OK.

Variation: Rotate the photo precisely before cropping

Sometimes you may want more control and precision when straightening your photo. The measure tool and Info palette can help you determine exactly how much rotation is required, eliminating the guesswork involved when rotating by sight.

 Identify a reference line in your photo. Look at your photo and try to identify an object or detail that should be oriented horizontally or vertically. This could be a horizon line, a pole, or the edge of a building, for example.

Measure the amount of rotation. Select the measure tool ( ). Position the pointer near the beginning of your reference, press Shift, and drag in a straight horizontal or vertical line. Then release Shift and drag the end of the line until it is aligned with your reference.

Rotate the photo. Choose Image > Rotate Canvas > Arbitrary and accept the values that appear in the dialog box.

Then continue to crop the photo using the crop tool.

Color-correct the photo

Scanners and other capture devices can sometimes introduce color casts, incorrect contrast levels, and other tonal irregularities into an image. Fortunately, many of these problems can be fixed or minimized by using Photoshop.

The color and tonal correction features in the Image > Adjust menu let you directly adjust the pixel values in a photo. You can also apply most of these corrections to an adjustment layer, which adjusts the photo without changing its pixel values permanently. You can discard the adjustment layer at any time to revert to the original, unadjusted photo.

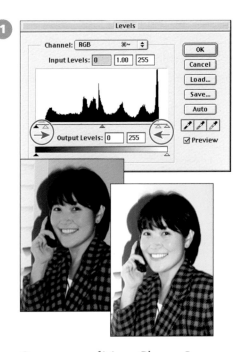

1

• To adjust the midtones, drag the gray rectangle to the left or right as desired.

You can also access the Levels dialog box by choosing Image > Adjust > Levels.

2

Correct tonalities. Choose Layer > New > Adjustment Layer, and choose Levels for the type. The Levels dialog box displays a histogram that represents the range of tonal levels in the image. You adjust tones by dragging the sliders directly under the histogram and previewing the change in your image:

• To adjust the shadows (dark tones), drag the black slider to the right until it is positioned under where the histogram pixels begin.

• To adjust the highlights (light tones), drag the white slider to the left until it is positioned under where the histogram pixels end.

Correct color casts. If your photo contains an unwanted color tint, you may have experienced color shifting as a result of lighting conditions during the photo shoot. The following are some typical lighting conditions, along with the color shifts they may cause.

Fluorescent light may cause a green cast. Add magenta to balance.

Tungsten bulb may cause a yellow cast. Add blue to balance.

Outdoor shade may cause a blue cast. Add yellow to balance.

To compensate for undesired color casts, select the Background in the Layers palette, and choose Image > Adjust > Variations. Select Midtones, and experiment with clicking different thumbnails to add more of a particular color to the balance, leaving the Variations dialog box open for step 3.

• To compare the adjusted image to the original, refer to the thumbnails at the top left. To revert to the original image, click the Original thumbnail.

• To adjust the amount of difference between each color variation, drag the slider at the top right.

Keep the Variations dialog box open for the next step.

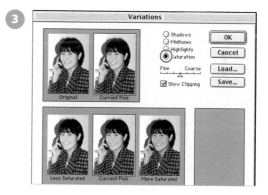

Adjust color saturation. If the colors in the photo appear dull, click Saturation in the Variations dialog box, and make the desired adjustment.

Sharpen details

Most scanned photos can be improved by using the Unsharp Mask filter to sharpen the image details. It's usually a good idea to apply this filter as the final step of your photo correction, especially if you've adjusted the resolution of the photo.

1 **Set the zoom to 100%.** Double-click the zoom tool (Q) to set the photo to 100% magnification.

Sharpen the photo. Choose Filter > Sharpen > Unsharp Mask. Drag the Amount slider until the photo is sufficiently sharp. Pay attention to detailed areas such as hair, eyes, and foliage, which can benefit dramatically from sharpening. However, be careful not to oversharpen, to avoid adding a grainy texture to smooth areas such as skin tones or blue skies.

Save the photo

Choose File > Save As, rename the file, and save it in Photoshop format.

You can now use the corrected photo in the project of your choice.

DESIGN TIP: How to take better photos

Sometimes you may want to shoot your own photos instead of searching for the appropriate image among available stock photos. A lively, well-taken photo of an interesting subject can help personalize your project and reduce the amount of "fix-up" time you spend in Photoshop. Here are a few basic photo-shooting tips to help you take good, well-composed photographs.

When shooting action shots, anticipate the peak moment, and take a variety of photos from different angles. Go ahead and take extra shots in case some don't turn out as you expected.

Experiment with different camera angles and perspectives. For example, crouch low to the ground to simulate a child's perspective, or shoot from a higher elevation for a bird's-eye view.

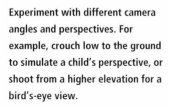

To create a more dynamic composition, shoot the subject against a neutral, solid background. To show the subject in relation to the surrounding environment, shoot from a farther distance.

Getting Your Photos Ready for Projects   11

Tools:

Adobe Photoshop

Materials:

Your photo

Project 1

Making Your Foreground Subject Stand Out

Blur or edit a photo background to focus attention on the subject.

An easy way to add focus to a photo is to change the texture of the background so that the foreground subject stands out. With the Photoshop Quick Mask feature, you can carefully isolate the foreground subject and apply edits to the rest of the photo.

❶ Getting started. In Photoshop, open your photo file.

❷ Switch to Quick Mask mode. Click the Quick Mask mode button (⬜) in the toolbox. In Quick Mask mode, you define selections by painting in the image.

Select the zoom tool (🔍), and click to zoom in on the edge of the foreground subject.

Set painting options. Click the Default Colors icon (◨) in the toolbox to set the foreground and background colors to black and white, respectively. Then select the paintbrush tool (✎). In the Options palette, set the opacity to 100% and the mode to Normal.

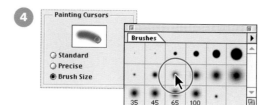

Set pointer and brush options. Choose File > Preferences > Display & Cursors. Under Painting Cursors, select Brush Size. This option displays the tool pointer as the current brush shape, allowing you to paint with greater precision.

In the Brushes palette, select a medium-sized, soft-edged brush.

Paint along the mask edges. Begin painting along the inside edge of the foreground subject. The soft-edged brush paints with a diffused, semi-transparent quality along the edges, which helps to make the boundary of the red mask less abrupt. This will help the blur effect blend more naturally into the edges of the foreground subject.

DESIGN TIP: Using Quick Masks to make selections

Photoshop's Quick Mask feature gives you a convenient and accurate way to select irregularly shaped areas in your image. When you switch to Quick Mask mode, you can use the paintbrush tool to paint in (or paint out) areas inside the selection. A temporary colored overlay covers the unselected areas and exposes the selected areas of the image. When you turn off Quick Mask mode, the colored mask is replaced by the "marching ants" of a standard selection.

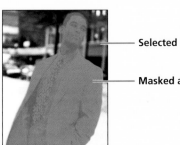

— Selected areas

— Masked areas

Paint with white to add areas to the selection (subtracting from the red overlay).

Resulting selection

Paint with black to remove areas from the selection (adding to the red overlay).

Resulting selection

Resulting selection

6

8

Paint inside the mask. When you've finished tracing the inside edge of the foreground subject, select a larger, hard-edged brush from the Brushes palette. Trace along the interior of the new inside edge. If you paint over an area by mistake, press X to toggle the foreground color to white, and "erase" the offending area. (Press X again to toggle back to black.)

Fine-tune the mask. Double-click the Quick Mask mode button (▣) in the toolbox, and choose a brighter, more contrasting color for the mask overlay. Use the paintbrush to fill any remaining "holes" in the mask.

When you finish, your foreground subject should appear evenly masked by the colored overlay.

7

9

Fill the interior of the mask. Make sure that the foreground color is set to black, and select the paint bucket tool (⊘). Click inside your foreground subject to fill the interior quickly with the red mask overlay.

Select the foreground subject. Click the Standard mode button (▢) in the toolbox to exit Quick Mask mode. The background area outside the mask should now be isolated as a selection. Choose Select > Inverse to select just the foreground subject.

10

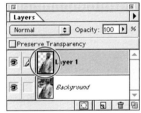

Isolate the foreground subject.
Choose Layer > New > Layer Via Copy
to place a copy of the foreground
subject on a new layer. In the Layers
palette, notice that the foreground
subject has been isolated from the
background.

11

Blur the background. In the Layers
palette, select the Background layer.
Choose Filter > Blur > Gaussian Blur
and drag the slider until you get the
desired effect. The blur affects only the
background because the foreground
subject has been isolated on a separate
overlying layer.

12 **Save working and export versions of
the photo.** To save a layered working
version, choose File > Save As, rename
the file, and save it in Photoshop
format. To save a single-layer version
for export to another application,
choose File > Save a Copy, rename the
file, and save it in a format supported
by that application.

Variation: Apply different filters to the background

There's no reason to limit yourself to
the Gaussian Blur filter in step 11.
Experiment with different filters, such
as Filter > Distort > Diffuse Glow or
Filter > Blur > Radial Blur.

Variation: Adjust the color of the background

Another way to alter the background is to change its color. Instead of using the Gaussian Blur filter in step 11, try applying Image > Adjust > Color Balance, Brightness/Contrast, or Hue/Saturation. Or create a neutral black-and-white background by choosing Image > Adjust > Desaturate.

Variation: Replace the background with a different image

Yet another way to emphasize the foreground is to replace the background area with another image. For best results, the replacement image should have the same (or larger) dimensions as the photo containing the original background.

1 **Select the background.** Make active the photo containing the original background. In the Layers palette, select the Background layer.

Add a new background. Open the image that you want to use as the replacement background, and arrange the two image windows side by side. Select the move tool (▶♦) and drag and drop the new background into your original photo window.

Reposition the new background. Make the original photo active, and use the move tool to position the new background as desired.

Tools:

Adobe Photoshop

Materials:

Your photo

Project 2

Coloring Photographs by Hand

Use the Photoshop painting features to give your photos a hand-colored look.

By removing a photo's original color, you can turn the photo into a template for your creative painting ideas. Fill the image with eye-catching hues, accentuate key details, and dab on your favorite color combinations.

Getting started. In Photoshop, open your photo file.

Prepare the image for coloring.
If you are working with a color image, choose Image > Adjust > Desaturate to remove the color from the photo. The photo now looks black and white.

If you are working with a grayscale image, choose Image > Mode > RGB Color. This converts the image to a mode that supports color.

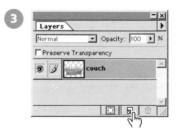

Create a new layer. Click the New Layer button (⬚) at the bottom of the Layers palette to create a new layer.

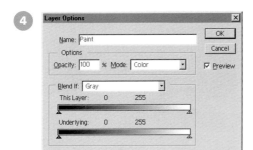

4

Set layer options. Double-click the new layer in the palette and give the layer a descriptive name. For Mode, choose Color. The colors that you paint will rest on this layer.

5

Specify painting settings. Select the paintbrush tool (✐). In the Brushes palette, click to select a medium-sized brush for painting.

6

Select a color. In the Color palette, drag across the color bar to sample different colors. When the color you want appears in the box at the upper left of the palette, release the mouse button to select the color.

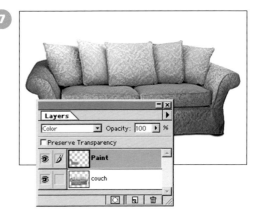

7

Paint the photo. Make sure that the new layer is selected in the Layers palette, and drag to paint color on the photo. (You may want to zoom in on the target area of the photo.) You can adjust settings to paint with greater precision:

• To have Photoshop show the size and shape of the brush tip you are using, choose File > Preferences > Display & Cursors. Under Painting Cursors, select Brush Size.

• To paint with a smaller brush tip, select the brush from the Brushes palette.

8

Correct your mistakes. If you paint over an unwanted area, choose Edit > Undo to reverse your mistake. Or select the eraser tool (⌫), select an appropriate brush tip from the Brushes palette, and drag to erase the offending color from the photo.

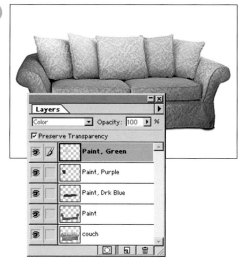

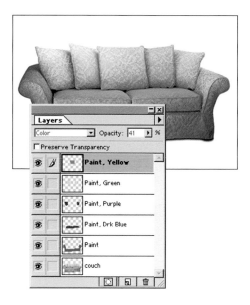

Add additional colors. Continue to paint your photo with different colors and brush tips.

For added control in painting, create a separate new layer for each color you paint in the photo. This method lets you apply different opacities, blending modes, and other effects to individual colors.

Save working and export versions of the photo. To save a layered working version, choose File > Save As, rename the file, and save it in Photoshop format. To save a single-layer version for export to another application, choose File > Save a Copy, rename the file, and save it in a format supported by that application.

Variation: Create a sepia-toned photo

This variation gives your photo a dusky brown, aged quality.

Set default colors. After desaturating your photo in step 2 of the project, click the Default Colors icon (■) in the toolbox to set the foreground color to black.

Create the sepia-toned effect. Choose Layer > New > Adjustment Layer and choose Hue/Saturation for Type. In the Hue/Saturation dialog box, select Colorize and drag the Hue and Saturation sliders to achieve a brownish tone.

By experimenting with different painting techniques, you can achieve original hand-colored effects.

Nobody said that you had to paint within the lines! Break out of the solid lines to create your own accents of color.

Use colors that work well with each other and with the image content. For examples, see "Preparing a Posterized Image for Print" on page 86.

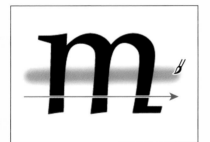

If you are painting different colors on a single layer, set the blending mode to Behind in the Paintbrush Options palette. This will keep the different colors from interfering with one another.

You can hand-paint just one detail or object in your photo to highlight it.

Tools:

Adobe Photoshop

Adobe PageMaker

Materials:

Border templates

Brochure template

Your photo

Project 3

Adding Borders to Photos

Add stylized borders that frame and accent your photos.

RUIS INVESTMENT

BECAUSE TIME IS MONEY

At Ruis Investments, we know how hard you work for your money. That's why we provide the largest and most comprehensive training programs for our employees. We offer knowledge-able, affordable financial guidance on all aspects of your investment portfolios. After all, we're only as successful as our clients.

Ruis Investments will help you build portfolios that are most suitable for your lifestyle.

Great Sand Dunes
National Monument

In a corner of the remote high-mountain San Luis Valley in the Colorado Rockies rise the Great Sand Dunes, the tallest dunes in North America. From billions of tiny grains of sand, these dunes have been built to heights of nearly 750 feet by winds that blow across the valley. The dunes cover approximately 39 square miles. But to under-stand the immensity of the dunes you don't really need facts and figures. Just walk in the dunes for a while.

Border patterns provide a subtle and easy way to add a handmade touch to your photos. To create a quick framing effect, just copy your photo into a premade border template, and then place the result into the brochure template.

This project provides step-by-step instructions for adding a border to a photo you plan to print. You can use the variations that follow to decorate or create your own border, or to add a border to an online photo.

① **Getting started.** In Photoshop, open your photo file.

② **Crop and resize the photo.** Crop and resize the photo to a height of 3 inches, a width of 3 inches, and a resolution of 200 pixels/inch (see "Crop and refine the photo size" on page 6 for instructions).

Your photo is now resized for use with the border and brochure templates.

③ **Open a border template.** Open one of the border templates in the Print folder inside the Proj03 folder. Choose a template suited to your output needs:

• Use templates P03a.psd through P03d.psd if you'll be placing your finished photo on a colored background for page layout.

• Use any template if you'll be placing your photo on a white background.

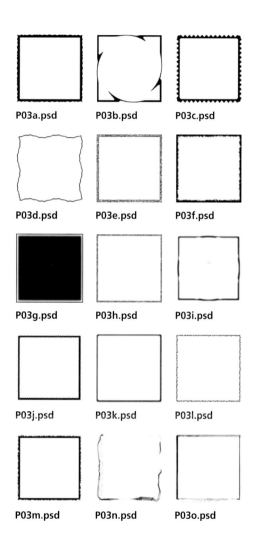

P03a.psd P03b.psd P03c.psd

P03d.psd P03e.psd P03f.psd

P03g.psd P03h.psd P03i.psd

P03j.psd P03k.psd P03l.psd

P03m.psd P03n.psd P03o.psd

Copy your photo to the border.
Arrange the two image windows so that they are both visible, and click your photo window to make it active.

Select the move tool (▸₊), and position the pointer over the photo. Hold down Shift and drag your photo onto the border image, releasing the mouse when the highlight appears in the border window.

Shift-dragging places a centered copy of your photo on top of the border. You won't see the border until you rearrange the layers in the next step.

 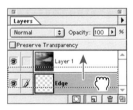

Reposition the layers. Click the border image window to make it active. In the Layers palette, drag the layer containing the border to the top of the layer list.

The border should now appear on top of your photo layer.

Save original and export versions of the border file. Make sure that the border image window is active. To save a layered working version, choose File > Save As, rename the file, and save it in Photoshop format. To save a single-layer version for export, choose File > Save a Copy, rename the file, and save it in TIFF format.

The TIFF version of the photo is now ready to be placed in the brochure template, P03.t65 in the Proj03 folder.

Variation: Resize the border to fit your photo

The project gives instructions on resizing your photo to fit the provided border templates. However, you may want to set your photo to a different width and height in step 2 of the project.

To resize the border to fit your photo, make the border image window active, choose Image > Image Size, and set the height and width to appropriate values. Then continue with step 4 of the project to copy your photo to the border window.

Variation: Add a border to an online photo

If you're planning to publish your photo online, use one of the low-resolution, Web-ready borders provided. You'll also want to save the final image as a JPEG or GIF, depending on the border template.

1 **Set the photo resolution.** Set the photo width and height as specified in step 2 of the project, but set the resolution to 72 pixels/inch.

2 **Open a low-resolution border file.** Open a border file in the Web folder. Choose a template suited to your output needs:

• Use templates P03a_w.psd through P03d_w.psd if you'll be placing your finished photo on a colored Web page background.

• Use any template if you'll be placing your photo on a white Web page background.

Continue with steps 4 and 5 of the project to copy your photo to the border file.

3 **Save working and Web versions of the file.** Save a layered Photoshop version as specified in step 6 of the project. Then save a version of the photo in a Web format:

• If you used templates P03a_w.psd through P03d_w.psd, choose Image > Mode > Indexed Color. For Palette, choose Adaptive, and for Dither, choose Diffusion. Then choose File > Export > GIF89a Export. For Transparency From, choose Alpha 1, and save the GIF file.

• If you used templates P03e_w.psd through P03o_w.psd, choose File > Save a Copy, rename the photo, and save it in JPEG or GIF format (see "Appendix: Choosing a File Format" on page 177).

Variation: Color the border

You can embellish many of the black-and-white border templates with your own colors. This variation can be applied to templates P03a.psd through P03d.psd, P03f.psd, and P03g.psd (in either the Print or Web folder).

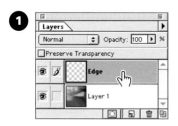

Select the border layer. After rearranging the layers in step 5 in the project, select the border layer in the Layers palette.

Turn on Preserve Transparency. Select Preserve Transparency in the Layers palette. This option lets you apply edits to the border layer without affecting the rest of the image.

Paint the border. Choose the foreground color you want to use. Then press Alt+Backspace (Windows) or Option+Delete (Mac OS) to fill the border with the new foreground color.

Variation: Create your own border

Instead of using the provided templates, you can create your border by adding a new layer directly to your photo. This way, you can add a custom border without having to resize your original photo.

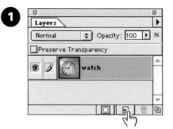

Create a new layer. After opening your photo in step 1 of the project, select the topmost layer in the Layers palette. Then click the New Layer button at the bottom of the palette to add a new layer to your photo.

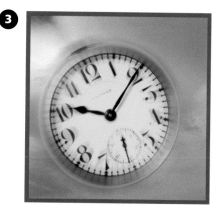

Define the border area. Choose Select > All to select the entire area of your new layer. Select the rectangular marquee tool (⬚), hold down Alt (Windows) or Option (Mac OS), and drag in the photo to select the interior area you want framed by the border. To reposition the selection rectangle as you draw, press the spacebar and drag with Alt or Option still depressed.

Holding down Alt or Option subtracts the interior area from the entire area, leaving just the border area selected.

Fill the selection. Choose the foreground color you want to use. Then press Alt+Backspace (Windows) or Option+Delete (Mac OS) to fill the border with the new foreground color.

Border created using Add Noise, Diffuse Glow, and Wave filters

Experiment with different filters. Choose commands from the Filter menu to apply a variety of artistic effects to your border. For example, the Torn Edges and Despeckle filters produce rougher edges, while the Angled Strokes and Crosshatch filters create more of a hand-drawn look.

Well-designed borders help to complement and frame your photo image, but sometimes you can have too much of a good thing! Overly colorful, large, or complex borders can produce results that are more gaudy than decorative, diverting attention from the image or message that you are trying to convey. To achieve balanced results with your photo borders, keep the following tips in mind.

When designing and decorating your border, remember that the focus of attention should be on the image, not the border. Keep your border down to a tasteful size, and try to avoid bright, oversaturated colors.

If you're placing the photo in a page-layout program, resist the temptation to add a keyline frame around the photo. Since your image already contains a stylized border, there's no need to outline it further.

Use a border style appropriate to your message or subject matter. For example, images with historical or traditional content are well-matched with more ornate borders, while streamlined borders are better suited to contemporary images.

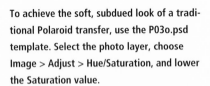

To achieve the soft, subdued look of a traditional Polaroid transfer, use the P03o.psd template. Select the photo layer, choose Image > Adjust > Hue/Saturation, and lower the Saturation value.

When you export a Photoshop image to another application or for the Web, you are essentially exporting the entire rectangular area of the image. This can result in an unwanted background if the image you intend to display is nonrectangular. What you need is a way to keep the background area transparent, so that your foreground shape displays seamlessly. Fortunately, Photoshop provides features that address this need.

Preserving transparency for printed output

To preserve background transparency when placing a Photoshop image in a page-layout application, use a clipping path. A clipping path traces the edge of your foreground image, acting as a "cookie cutter" that allows only the interior of the path to print. To export a file containing a clipping path, save the file in TIFF format (for output on an inkjet or laser printer) or Photoshop EPS format (for output on a PostScript® laser printer).

This project provides templates that already contain clipping paths. For instructions on creating your own clipping paths, see "Variation: Select your own area to be clipped" on page 140; also see "Variation: Draw your own path" on page 141.

Great Sand Dunes
National Monument

Great Sand Dunes
National Monument

Artwork with and without clipping path

Preserving transparency for online output

To preserve background transparency when placing your image on a Web page, use the GIF89a Export command to save the image in GIF format. Unlike JPEG, GIF lets you define transparent areas in your image so that the image appears as a nonrectangular shape on a Web page background.

The GIF format recognizes transparency information stored in an alpha channel. Like a clipping path, an alpha channel defines the edge of your foreground subject. This project provides templates that already contain transparency alpha channels.

Great Sand Dunes
National Monument

Great Sand Dunes
National Monument

Artwork with and without transparency

Project 3: Adding Borders to Photos   31

Tools:

Adobe Photoshop

Adobe PageMaker

Materials:

Newsletter template

Your photos

Project 4

Using Photographs in Newsletters

Prepare your color photos for black-and-white reproduction or two-color printing in a newsletter.

ZZZinsider

THE SLEEP INDUSTRY SPECIALISTS   *Spring Edition*

NEW FACES

Liz Budo appointed to Board of Directors

The stock price soared last month in response to the anticipated appointment of Liz Budo to the Board of Directors of ZZZ company. Liz joined ZZZ last November as Senior Vice President for Corporate Development. She flew in to the Detroit office just long enough to accept the appointment before she was whisked away to Headquarters to meet with the Chairman of the Board.

Liz most recently worked at Snore, Inc. in Minneapolis, where she was head of the product development. One of her more notable accomplishments at Snore was to establish a venture capital fund to foster development of new technology in the industry. When Liz started the Fund in 1990, she based it on a philosophy that continues to guide Snore, Inc. in managing their fund today: Deliver consistent performance with limited risk. That firm belief helped the Snore fund to succeed.

This Quarter

New appointment to Board of Directors.

Product line expands to include featherbeds.

Company picnic planned for August on Farallon Islands.

Write to us at editor@zzz.com.

Company picnic planned for August

If you ve just recently joined the staff at ZZZ Company, you may not have heard yet about our company picnics.

Some company picnics have given the word picnic a bad name. They make you think of going to the same park every summer, drinking a beer, eating some potato salad and a hot dog, and standing around, trying to think of something to say to your fellow employees. You stand around for awhile, maybe walk over and watch the raffle going on at the stage nearby, say Hi to a couple of employees and try to remember their

Bob takes the Surfing trophy

names, eat some dessert, and then you go home. Sound like fun? Well, if this is what you re expecting to sign up for at the summer picnic this August, you ll be disappointed.

To give you an idea of what ZZZ company picnics are like, let s talk about the last few picnics. Ask John Peppersmith to tell you about the sunburn he got while sailing to the mysterious island somewhere in the Pacific. Ask Regimond Donaldson how he got that scratch on his leg while hiking through prickly brambles to the secluded waterfall. And ask Marylu Tallfeather about the giant fossil egg that s displayed on her desk. But don t worry. They still got to eat hot dogs and drink beer.

Here is a quick technique for converting your color photos into grayscale images for a newsletter. You can also use a duotone variation to create two-color images. A PageMaker template for a newsletter is supplied, but is not required for this project.

Open your photo. In Photoshop, open your scanned color photo.

Getting started. Determine what photos you want to use and what size you want them to be on your final newsletter page. The resolution of each final image should be at least 300 pixels per inch (see "Scan the photo at the correct size" on page 4).

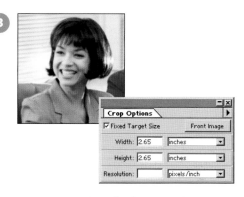

Crop or resize the image. Crop your image to the size you want or, if you want to make the entire image smaller, choose Image > Image Size and enter the dimensions. For tips on cropping and image resizing, see "Crop and refine the photo size" on page 6.

The front page of the newsletter template has placeholders for an image 2.65 inches wide by 2.65 inches high and a second image 1.69 inches wide by 1.69 inches high.

4 **Convert to grayscale.** Choose Image > Mode > Grayscale and click OK to discard the color information. (Before you convert your color image to grayscale, you may want to save a color version of the file.)

5

Adjust the tonal range and sharpen. If you need to adjust the shadows, highlights, or gray midtones, choose Image > Adjust > Levels. For information on adjusting the tonal range, see "Correct tonalities" on page 8.

To sharpen the image, choose Filter > Sharpen > Unsharp Mask. Drag the Amount slider until the image is sufficiently sharp. Pay attention to detailed areas such as hair, eyes, and foliage, which can benefit dramatically from sharpening. However, be careful not to oversharpen, to avoid adding a grainy texture to smooth areas such as skin tones or blue skies.

6 **Save and place in a newsletter.** Choose File > Save and save your changes in Photoshop format. Then choose File > Save As, rename the file, and save the file in TIFF format. Place the image in a PageMaker document or other layout software. You can use the provided newsletter template P04.t65 as a starting point.

Variation: Create a duotone photo for two-color printing

Add a second ink color to your grayscale images to create duotones for a two-color newsletter.

1 **Open a grayscale photo.** Start with a grayscale image with good tonal range.

2 **Determine the ink color.** Determine the color of the second ink you'll use when printing your newsletter. (The first ink color should be black.) Most ink colors are specified using a color matching system, such as the PANTONE® Matching System. Your printer can help you choose a color that will work well both in text and as a duotone color for your photos.

3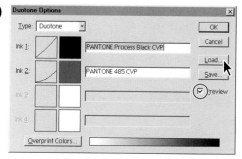

4

Grayscale   **Simulation of PANTONE 485 (red)**

Grayscale   **Duotone**

Process Cyan   **Process Yellow**

Convert the image to duotone.
Choose Image > Mode > Duotone.
(Note that color images must be converted to grayscale before Duotone mode becomes available.) In the Duotone Options dialog box, choose Duotone from the Type pop-up menu, select Preview, and select a color for the second ink.

You can select the color by clicking the color box for Ink 2, choosing a book of custom colors from the pop-up menu, and then choosing a color. Or you can click the Load button and choose the color from a set of predefined duotones available in the Photoshop application folder.

Experiment. Try different colors to get an effect you like. When you're done, save the changes.

The first duotone example in these illustrations shows a simulation of the spot color red 485 bl 4, selected from the PANTONE Duotones folder (Adobe Photoshop 5.0\Goodies\ Duotone Presets\Duotones). The other duotone examples use process colors Cyan bl 3 and Yellow bl 3.

5 **Save an export version.** To save a version of the duotone image that can be color-separated when you print it, choose File > Save As, rename the file, and save the file in Photoshop EPS format. For Preview, choose a TIFF preview; for Encoding, choose ASCII (Windows) or Binary (Mac OS).

Any PANTONE color can be used as both a duotone ink for photos and as a spot color for text and graphics. The color you choose should be flexible enough to work in a variety of tint percentages or shades, so be sure to test a few colors in PageMaker by applying them to text and line art (such as rules or borders), in addition to previewing the effect on your duotone photos in Photoshop.

A good spot color (such as the spot color simulated here) works well with reverse type.

Choose a color dark enough to be used for type as well as for photos.

Beware of light colors such as yellow, orange, cyan, or magenta, which may disappear at tints less than 80%.

You can print test pages of your two-color newsletter to a color laser or inkjet printer, but the best way to ensure that you know what your page will look like when printed in ink on a printing press is to have a high-resolution contact color proof made at a service bureau.

If there is text or artwork in your newsletter that will be printed using the same second ink color used in your photos, it's important that they be named exactly the same in both your page-layout program and in your Photoshop file before you have the proof made. This ensures that all elements on your page containing the same spot color will print on a single piece of film. Most layout applications will display the second color in the color list once the duotone photo has been placed, making it easy to select the same color when painting text or other graphics. Colors may not display identically in different applications. The important thing is to make sure that they are named consistently in each file.

Images that don't produce good duotones include line or clip art, very high-contrast grayscale photos, photos that are already in Bitmap mode, and artwork or photos that are very dark or black to begin with.

Tools:

Adobe Photoshop

Adobe PageMaker

Materials:

Masthead templates

Newsletter template

Your logo

Project 5

Creating a Masthead for a Newsletter

Use type layer effects to create an impressive masthead for your company newsletter.

Integrate your company logo with the included Photoshop template to create a grayscale masthead with special type layer effects. Then place the masthead in your newsletter. A PageMaker template is provided for a black-and-white newsletter to be printed at approximately 1200 dpi. Also included are Photoshop templates for creating duotone and full-color mastheads.

1 **Getting started.** In Photoshop, open the P05a.psd or P05b.psd masthead template in the Proj05 folder.

The dimensions of the masthead are 7.5 by 1.125 inches, designed to fit the title space in the PageMaker newsletter template. If your newsletter title will occupy a smaller or larger space, you can use the Canvas Size command to change the masthead dimensions.

2

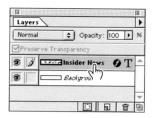

Add your own title. In the Layers palette, double-click the type layer, select the text, and type a new title. If desired, choose a different typeface. (The typeface in these illustrations is

76-point ITC Esprit Bold.) Be sure to leave room for your company logo to be placed to the left of the title. For tips on choosing typefaces, see "Using type in newsletters" on page 42.

Note that with large titles like this one, uneven space between letters becomes more obvious. Click between the letters where kerning is necessary and enter new values in the Kern text box.

3 **Adjust the layer effects.** Notice that when you changed the title, the type retained the beveled edge and drop shadow effects that were on the original text. To adjust the effects, make the type layer active and choose Layer > Effects > Drop Shadow. Experiment with the settings. Be sure to run a hard-copy proof of the effects at the same printer resolution you'll use when printing your newsletter.

4 Insider News

Add your logo. Choose File > Place and select your logo file. Resize your logo as needed by Shift-dragging a corner handle, and position the logo to the left of the title. Double-click in the image to rasterize and place the logo.

(5) **Apply the type layer effects to your logo.** In the Layers palette, select the type layer and choose Layer > Effects > Copy Effects. Then select the logo layer and choose Layer > Effects > Paste Effects.

(6) **Add a background texture.** This step is optional. Some layer effects work better when there is an image behind the type. Try adding your own background texture to the masthead by placing an image on a layer beneath the type layer.

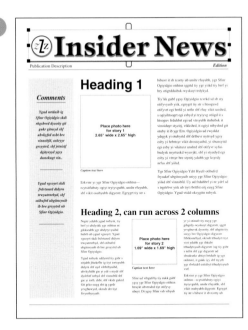

(7) **Save and place the masthead in the newsletter.** Choose File > Save As and save a working version of the masthead in Photoshop format. Then choose File > Save a Copy, rename the file, and save it in TIFF format.

In PageMaker, open the template P05.t65 in the Proj05 folder. Select the placeholder frame at the top of the newsletter and choose File > Place. Accept the current settings and place the TIFF version of the masthead image. Click Yes to include the masthead as part of the newsletter file.

Variation: Adjust layer effects for two-color or full-color mastheads

Experiment with different layer effects on mastheads for two-color or full-color newsletters. Two additional Photoshop templates are provided as starting points.

1

Experiment with effects for a duotone masthead. If you have a second ink color available for printing your newsletter, in Photoshop, open the file P05c.psd in the Proj05 folder. Choose Image > Mode > Duotone and specify the color you're using. Photoshop layer effects will incorporate the color into the shadows and highlights, depending on the settings you use.

In the Layers palette, select the type layer. Choose Layer > Effects > Drop Shadow and experiment with the settings for different effects.

2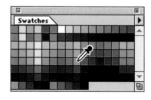

Experiment with effects for a full-color masthead. In Photoshop, open the file P05d.psd in the Proj05 folder. This color image provides an additional range of layer effects.

Click a color in the Swatches palette or click the Foreground Color box in the toolbox and select a new foreground color. Press Alt+Backspace (Windows®) or Option+Delete (Mac OS) to fill the type with the selected color. Then, with the type layer active, choose Layer > Effects > Drop Shadow and experiment with the settings for different effects. To fill the logo with the current foreground color, select the logo's layer in the Layers palette and press Alt+Backspace (Windows) or Option+Delete (Mac OS).

3 **Save an export version.** Save a version of the duotone or full-color image that can be color separated when you print it. Choose File > Save As, rename the file, and save the file in Photoshop EPS format. For Preview, choose a TIFF preview; for Encoding, choose ASCII (Windows) or Binary (Mac OS).

The newsletter and masthead templates in the Productivity Kit use basic fonts such as Times and Helvetica. Here are some tips for choosing and using type in your newsletters.

(A) **Masthead**: The title of your newsletter should be distinctive and attention-getting. Choose a typeface that is different from other headings in your publication. At this size, you can use a stylish, decorative typeface.

(B) **Text**: Serif typefaces such as Garamond, Palatino, or Minion are readable for longer bodies of text. Ten points is a good type size. Avoid 12 points for text! It's too big.

(C) **Captions**: An italic or bold italic version of the text font is a safe bet for captions (7 to 9 points work well). A good design guideline is to vary the font, size, and weight of neighboring type.

INSIDER NEWS

THE SLEEP INDUSTRY SPECIALISTS *Spring Edition*

(D) ## NEW FACES

Liz Budo appointed to Board of Directors

The stock price soared last month in response to the anticipated appointment of Liz Budo to the Board of Directors of ZZZ company. Liz joined ZZZ last November as Senior Vice President for Corporate Development. She flew in to the Detroit office just long enough to accept the appointment before she was whisked away to Headquarters to meet with the Chairman of the Board.

Liz most recently worked at Snore, Inc. in Dallas. As head of the product development she established a venture capital fund to foster development of new technology in the industry.

Company picnic planned for August

If you've just recently joined the staff at ZZZ Company, you may not have heard yet about our company picnics.

Some company picnics have given the word "picnic" a bad name. They make you think of going to the same park every summer, drinking a beer, eating some potato salad and a hot dog, and standing around, trying to think of something to say to your fellow employee who's standing next to you. You stand around for awhile, maybe walk over and watch the raffle going on at the stage nearby, say "Hi" to a couple of employees and try to remember their names, eat some dessert, and then you go home. Sound like fun? Well, if this is what you're expecting to sign up for this August, you'll be disappointed.

To give you an idea of what ZZZ company picnics are like, let's talk about the last few picnics. Ask John Peppersmith to tell you about the sunburn he got while sailing to the mysterious island somewhere in the Pacific. Ask Regimond Donaldson how he got that scratch on his leg while hiking through prickly brambles to the secluded waterfall. And ask Marylu Tallfeather about the giant fossil egg that's displayed on her desk in a glass c(E)t don't worry. They still eat hot dogs and drink beer.

Every year CPC (Company Picnic Committee) meets in secret to plan a new and exciting picnic experience. The rules are that the picnic must involve food, which is hauled in various sized "picnic baskets" to a chosen location, and the location must be different than the years before (unless there was a petition to repeat a particularly popular one).

(D) **Headings**: Sans serif typefaces, such as Univers, Frutiger, or Eurostyle, work well because they have a condensed font as well as a good range of weights (semibold, bold, and black.

Avoid underlines and italics in headings. Instead, use the weight and size of the typeface to create visual hierarchy on the page. Or use the text font in a larger size and bolder weight as an alternative heading style.

(E) **Paragraph breaks**: Use the Space Before or Space After Paragraph option in your page-layout program instead of double returns to create space between paragraphs.

Tools:

Adobe Photoshop

Adobe PageMaker

Materials:

Slide template

Your photo

Project 6

Creating a Photographic Background for a Slide Presentation

Use Photoshop layers to create striking backdrops for slide presentations.

Add flair to your presentations by using a photograph as a slide background. Photographic backdrops help frame and add thematic focus to presentation text, and your audience will appreciate the subtle graphic variety. You can edit and save your backdrop in Photoshop and then finish the slide in a presentation application, or you can use the provided template to create a PDF slide.

1 **Getting started.** In Photoshop, open your photo file.

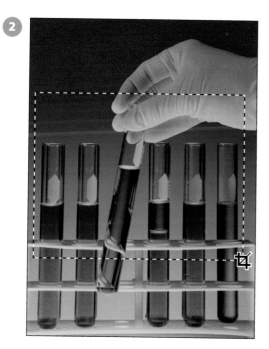

Crop and resize the photo. Crop and resize the photo to a height of 480 pixels, a width of 640 pixels, and a resolution of 72 pixels/inch

(see "Getting Your Photos Ready for Projects" on page 2). These values will produce full-screen slides for display on a monitor or online projector.

3 **Add a new layer.** In the Layers palette, Alt-click (Windows) or Option-click (Mac OS) the New Layer button (▣), and add a new layer named **Container**.

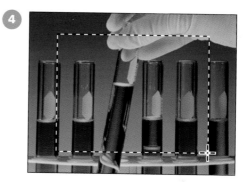

Draw the text container. Select the rectangular marquee tool (▣) and drag in the image to draw a rectangular border. Drag inside the border to reposition it.

You'll make the area within this border a tinted, semitransparent backdrop for your slide text.

⑤

Fill the container with white. To fill the container, choose Edit > Fill. For Contents, choose White and make sure that Opacity is set to 100% and Mode to Normal.

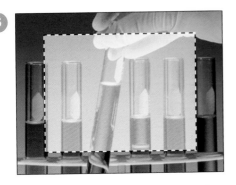

⑥

Screen back the container. In the Layers palette, make sure the Container layer is selected and lower its Opacity setting. Use a setting that will let you easily read the text that will be placed on top.

⑦ **Save working and export versions of the photo.** To save a layered working version, choose File > Save As, rename the file, and save it in Photoshop format. To save a single-layer version for export, choose File > Save a Copy, rename the file, and save it in TIFF format (for export to the provided slide template) or in a format supported by your presentation application.

It's good practice to save a working version of the photo in Photoshop format, so that you can readjust the opacity and placement of the container at any time. For instructions on how to use the provided slide template, see "Creating finished slides from the background" on page 50.

Variation: Draw different container shapes

There's no reason to confine your text to square regions. For a graphical twist, place your text inside ovals or hand-drawn shapes. After creating a new layer in step 3 of the project, use another tool such as the elliptical marquee (○), lasso (♡), or polygon lasso (♡) tool to draw your container. Then continue with step 5 of the project to fill the container.

Variation: Transform the container

Here is a quick way to rotate or distort a rectangular container while centering it in the photo area.

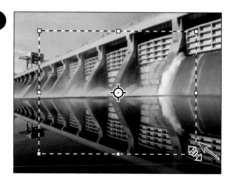

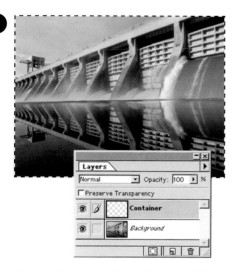

Select the layer boundaries. After creating a new layer in step 3 of the project, make sure the new layer is selected and choose Select > All. This selects the rectangular border of the layer, which you can transform and use as your text container.

Transform the container. Choose Select > Transform Selection and transform the container:

• To scale and center the container, hold down Alt (Windows) or Option (Mac OS) and drag a handle.

• To rotate, place the pointer outside the bounding box and drag.

• To distort freely, press Control (Windows) or Command (Mac OS) and drag a handle.

• To skew, press Control+Shift (Windows) or Command+Shift (Mac OS) and drag a side handle.

• To apply perspective, press Control+Alt+Shift (Windows) or Command+Option+Shift (Mac OS) and drag a corner handle.

• To undo the last handle adjustment, choose Edit > Undo.

Press Enter to apply the transformation. Press Esc to cancel the transformation.

Continue with step 5 in the project to fill the container.

Variation: Soften the container edges

Blurring gives your text containers a softer, more gradual border. After you screen back the container in step 6 of the project, choose Select > Deselect. Then choose Filter > Blur > Gaussian Blur, and drag the slider to soften the container edges.

Variation: Fill the container with a sampled color

If you'd like to tint the container with a color other than white in step 5, select the eyedropper tool (✐) and click to sample a color in the image. Then choose Edit > Fill and for Contents, choose Foreground Color.

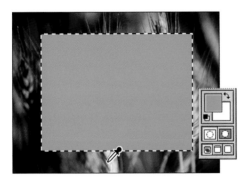

Variation: Create multiple containers

Now that you've developed a knack for text containers, why not create more than one per slide? Add separate containers for presentation heads, charts, or numbering schemes. As always, don't overdo it. Well-placed containers add emphasis, not clutter, to your presentation points.

After screening back the first container in step 6 of the project, repeat steps 3 through 6 of the project as needed, adding additional layers and drawing additional containers over different parts of the image. Try experimenting with different tints and blending modes (chosen from the menu in the Layers palette) for the new containers.

When choosing a background photograph, look for images that contain interesting subject matter related to your presentation topic. Use neutral colors to fill the container. (Bright colors make it difficult to read overlying text.) White fills are effective, because they act as subtle tints of the original colors in the image.

Avoid placing the container in awkward locations, such as directly over a subject's face.

Don't place the container too low in the slide area. You might cause the slide to appear lopsided or cut off when projected.

Place the container in the center of the image area or higher. Choose View > Show Rulers to display measurement guides.

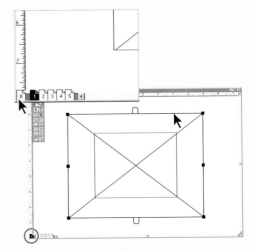

When creating your slide background, keep in mind the final medium of the slide presentation. Online slides, for example, require settings different from those used by traditional photographic slides.

Getting your slide background ready for a service bureau

If you plan to have your slides generated at a service bureau, check with the bureau for the recommended dimensions, resolution, and file format.

Creating PDF slides

By importing your background into the PageMaker slide template, you can add your own text and graphics, and export the resulting slides as a PDF file.

To use the PageMaker slide template:

1 In PageMaker, open P06.t65 in the Proj06 folder.

2 Click the master-page icon to view to the template master page. Select the outer rectangular frame in the page.

3 Choose File > Place. Leave the place options at their current settings, select the TIFF version of your slide background, and click Place. Click Yes to include the slide background as part of the file.

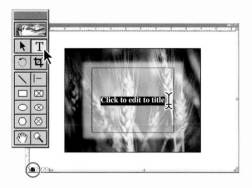

Importing your slide background into Microsoft PowerPoint

By importing your slide background into Microsoft® PowerPoint, you can add formatted presentation points to complete the slide.

To import your slide background into Microsoft PowerPoint:

1 With your PowerPoint presentation open, choose Format > Background and then choose Fill Effects from the pop-up menu.

2 Click the Picture tab and then click Select Picture.

3 Select your slide background file.

4 Turn to the first publication page, and replace the sample text with your own text, moving or resizing the frames as needed. Use the premade styles in the Styles palette to format the text. You can also import a graphic into any frame by selecting the frame and choosing File > Place.

5 Continue to edit publication pages for additional slides, duplicating or deleting pages as needed. You can also create new master pages for any additional slide backgrounds you would like to use.

6 Choose File > Export > Adobe PDF.

7 In Acrobat, open the PDF file you exported. Acrobat provides a number of useful features for slide presentation, such as Full Screen view, page-by-page navigation, and the ability to add, delete, rearrange, and bookmark pages.

Tools:

Adobe Photoshop

Adobe PageMaker

Materials:

Sidebar templates

Texture actions

Slide template

Your photo

Project 7

Creating Photographic Sidebars for Slides

Use photos to create sidebar backdrops that frame your online presentations.

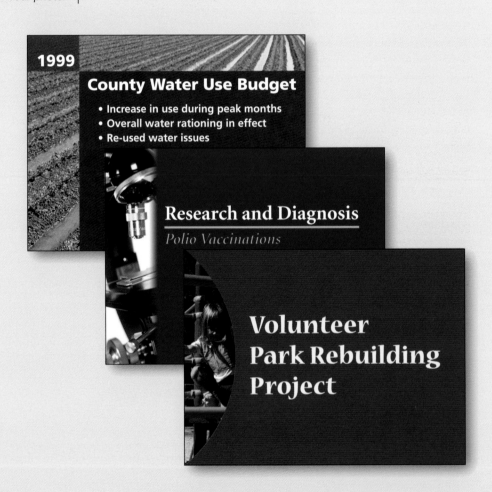

Photographic sidebars add visual flair to your presentations without stealing focus from the main text, graphs, or charts. The photo is visible only along the edges of the slide, leaving the center available for informational content. Using the provided sidebar templates, you can create a variety of backdrop and framing effects for online slides.

① **Getting started.** In Photoshop, open your photo file and open the sidebar template you want to use. The Proj07 folder contains 8 templates, each with a different sidebar shape and layout.

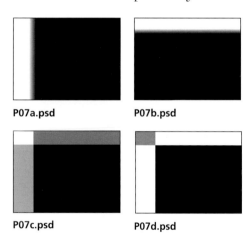

P07a.psd   P07b.psd

P07c.psd   P07d.psd

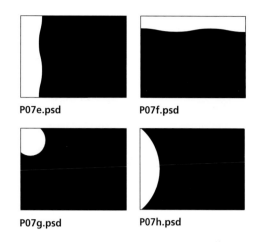

P07e.psd   P07f.psd

P07g.psd   P07h.psd

② **Crop and resize the photo.** Crop and resize the photo to at least 480 pixels high or 640 pixels wide, or both, depending on your template layout. Set the photo to a resolution of 72 pixels/inch (see "Getting Your Photos Ready for Projects" on page 2).

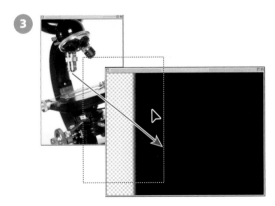

Copy the photo to the template.
Select the move tool (🔾) and drag the
photo into the sidebar template. When
the template window becomes
highlighted, release the mouse button
to drop a copy of the photo in the
window. To reposition the photo in the
template, drag with the move tool.

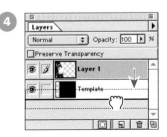

Rearrange layers. In the Layers
palette, drag the photo layer to the
bottom of the list.

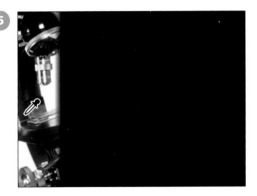

**Sample a color for the body of the
slide.** Select the eyedropper tool (🖋),
and click in the photo to sample a color
for the body of the slide.

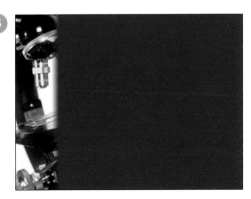

Color the slide body. In the Layers
palette, select the Template layer. Then
choose Edit > Fill, choose Foreground
Color for the contents, and click OK.

7 **Save working and export versions of the file.** To save a layered working version, choose File > Save As, rename the file, and save it in Photoshop format. To save a single-layer version for export, choose File > Save a Copy, rename the file, and save it in TIFF format (for export to the provided slide template) or in a format supported by your presentation application.

For instructions on how to use the provided slide template, see "Creating finished slides from the background" on page 50.

Variation: Flip the sidebar template

By changing the horizontal or vertical orientation of a template, you can create a variety of different looks. For example, you can make the sidebar area appear along the left or the right, or along the top or the bottom of the slide. After opening the template file in step 1, choose Image > Rotate Canvas > Flip Vertical or Flip Horizontal.

Original template   Flip Horizontal

Variation: Add texture to the sidebar template

Use the handy premade actions to add textured effects to your sidebar templates.

1

Load the actions. After coloring the slide body in step 6 of the project, choose Load Actions from the Actions palette menu. Select and open P07.atn in the Proj07 folder.

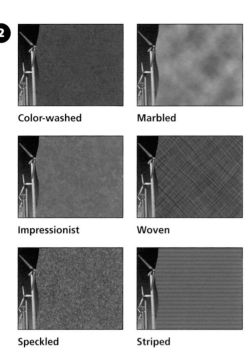

Color-washed   **Marbled**

Impressionist   **Woven**

Speckled   **Striped**

If you don't like the results of the action, use the History palette to return to the previous image state, or delete the Template copy layer in the Layers palette.

Play an action on the Template layer. Make sure that the Template layer is selected in the Layers palette. In the Actions palette, select the action you'd like to run, and click the Play button (▷).

When deciding on a color for the body of your slide, consider your presentation needs. Different body colors produce different display and reading effects.

Neutral, subdued colors promote the visibility of the slide contents and work well with the provided texture actions.

Bright, vivid colors may make text difficult to read.

Materials:

Your EPS logo

Slide template

Project 8

Embossing Your Logo on a Slide Background

Add business identity to your slide presentations by embossing your logo on a background.

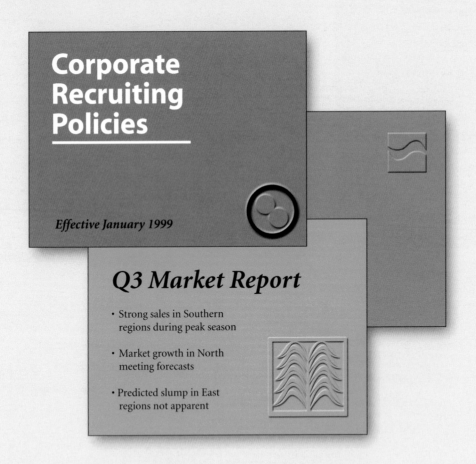

Photoshop makes it easy for you to enhance your artwork with effects such as drop shadows, three-dimensional bevels, or embossed edges. Using these *layer effects,* you can create an elegant embossed logo, which you can use as "stationery" for your online slide presentations.

To use this project, first create your logo in a graphics application such as Adobe Illustrator®, and save the logo in EPS format.

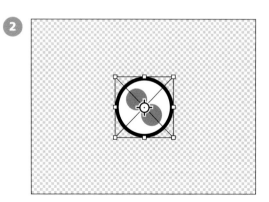

1 **Getting started.** In Photoshop, choose File > New. Set the width to 640 pixels, the height to 480 pixels, and the resolution to 72 pixels/inch. Make sure that Mode is set to RGB, and select Transparent for the Contents. Click OK to create the new Photoshop image that will serve as your slide background.

Place your logo. Choose File > Place, select your logo file, and click Place. The placed logo appears in the image with a bounding box and an X through it.

If you have trouble locating your logo file, it may not be saved in the correct format. Reopen the logo in the application used to create it, and save it as an EPS file.

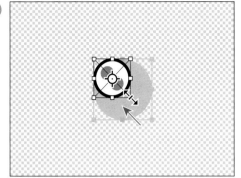

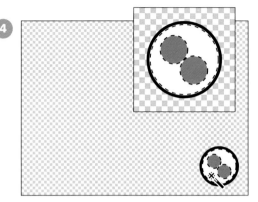

Adjust and position the logo. Do any of the following to adjust the logo:

• To scale the logo, drag one of the handles on the bounding box. To scale proportionally, hold down Shift and drag a corner handle.

• To rotate the logo, position the pointer outside the bounding box and drag.

• To reposition the logo, position the pointer inside the bounding box and drag.

• To cancel the placement and start over, press Esc.

When you are satisfied with the logo placement, press Enter to make the logo a permanent part of the image.

Remove unwanted areas of the logo. Examine your logo for filled areas that should appear transparent. For example, if your logo is doughnut-shaped, the center hole may be filled with white or another background color. You want this hole to appear transparent (filled with no color) so that the edges of the hole can be embossed along with the outside edges of the logo.

To remove unwanted filled areas, select the magic wand tool (✳\) and click one of the areas. Shift-click additional areas to select them as well; then press Backspace (Windows) or Delete (Mac OS) to remove the selected areas.

⑤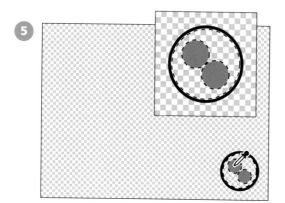

⑥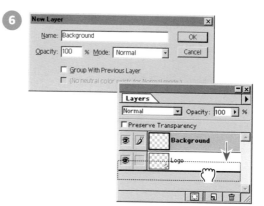

Choose a color for the background.
Select the eyedropper tool (🖋) and click in the logo to sample a color. This color will be used to fill the background, so that the logo appears stamped into the area behind it.

Create and fill the Background layer. In the Layers palette, Alt-click (Windows) or Option-click (Mac OS) the New Layer button (🔲), and create a new layer called **Background**. Drag the Background layer to the bottom of the Layers palette.

Press Alt+Backspace (Windows) or Option+Delete (Mac OS) to fill the background with the color you sampled from the logo. Don't worry if you can't see your logo at this point.

7

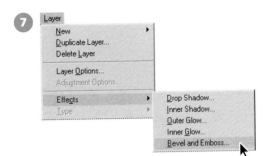

Emboss the logo. In the Layers palette, select the layer containing your logo. Choose Layer > Effects > Bevel and Emboss to preview and set your embossing options.

The default Emboss settings work nicely with most logos, but it's fun to experiment. When you're satisfied with the effect, click OK.

8 **Save working and export versions of the file.** To save a layered working version, choose File > Save, name the file, and save it in Photoshop format. To save a single-layer version for export, choose File > Save a Copy, rename the file, and save it in a TIFF format (for export to the provided slide template) or in a format supported by your presentation application.

Variation: Emboss clip art

Instead of embossing your logo, you can emboss clip art onto a background. Simple black-and-white clip art usually produces the best results.

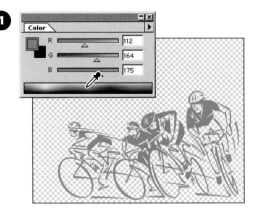

1 Fill the clip art. After removing unwanted areas in step 4 of the project, use the eyedropper tool or Color palette to choose a new color. In the Layers palette, select Preserve Transparency, and press Alt+Backspace (Windows) or Option+Delete (Mac OS) to fill the clip art with the new color.

2 Fill the Background layer. Continue with step 6 of the project to create a new Background layer, filling it with the same color.

The embossing effect can vary depending on the composition, shape, and color of your logo art. In general, you'll get good effects with logos that contain large, bold shapes. Try to avoid using logos that contain fine lines, since these lines may be obscured when you emboss them.

HUNTER GREENS
Garden Shops

Sometimes you can use just a detail of your logo for the embossing effect. Try to use the most graphically interesting part of the logo.

When you're working with a dark-colored logo and background, the emboss may not show up clearly. You can fix this by adjusting the emboss settings. In the Effects dialog box, choose a lighter color for the Shadow, lower the Opacity, or switch to a different mode such as Screen.

If you're using Illustrator 8 to create your logo, you can take advantage of several helpful features.

Cutting out transparent areas

You can use the Pathfinder palette to exclude areas in your logo that you want to appear transparent. The Pathfinder palette lets you "subtract" one shape from another, saving you the step of removing areas of the logo in Photoshop.

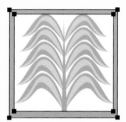

Select two objects.

Click the Minus Front button in the Pathfinder palette.

Foreground object is excluded from background object.

Creating a multilayered logo

By placing different parts of your logo on separate layers, you can create an attractive multilevel embossing effect.

To create a multilevel emboss:

1 In Illustrator 8, draw a rectangle with a width of 640 points and a height of 480 points, and color the rectangle. This represents the boundaries of your slide background.

2 Place different elements of your logo on separate layers using the Layers palette.

3 Choose File > Export and export the logo file in Photoshop 5 format. Set the color model to RGB and the resolution to Screen (72 dpi), and select Write Layers.

4 Open the logo file in Photoshop 5. Select each layer in turn, and apply an embossing effect. Try using different emboss settings for each layer.

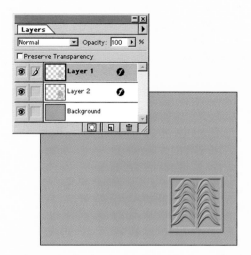

Project 9

Creating Postcards

Use your photos to create an appealing image for a 6-by-4.25-inch postcard.

Here's a technique for layering your photos and type to produce an attractive postcard image. Print the postcard from Photoshop or place the image in a PageMaker template designed to print as a two-sided postcard.

① **Getting started.** In Photoshop, open either the P09a.psd or P09b.psd file in the Proj09 folder. (If the blue guide-lines aren't visible, choose View > Show Guides.) Choose File > Save As and save the file with a different name.

P09a.psd

P09b.psd

②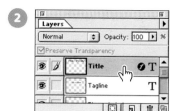

Customize the type. In the Layers palette, double-click the Title layer, select the type, and replace the words with your own. You can also change the font or size of the type.

③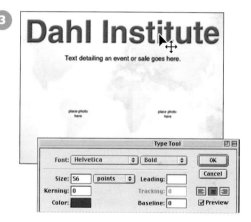

Reposition the type. You can reposition the type as needed while the Type Tool dialog box is still open. Simply move the pointer outside of the dialog box—the pointer changes to the move tool (▶₊)—and drag to reposition the type. Be sure to keep your type within the blue trim marks around the edge of the postcard.

4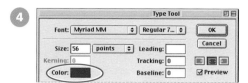

Change the color of the type. With the type selected in the Type Tool dialog box, click in the Color box and choose a color from the Color Picker dialog box or from the image itself. The pointer changes to the eyedropper tool (🖋) when it's outside the Color Picker.

Repeat steps 2, 3, and 4 for the type on the Tagline layer.

5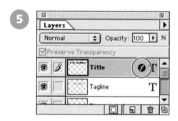

Adjust the title layer effects. In the Layers palette, double-click the layer effects icon (🄝) on the Title layer. Select the Preview option and edit the settings for the applied Drop Shadow effect, or deselect the Apply check box and choose a different effect from the pop-up menu. (The Drop Shadow, Outer Glow, and Bevel and Emboss effects work particularly well with these postcards.)

6

Determine the pixel dimensions of your photos. Open each photo that you're planning to add to the postcard image and check its dimensions. For best results, use images with dimensions of at least 300 by 450 pixels. (In this example, the photo is 2.25 inches wide, 1.5 inches high, and 200 pixels per inch in resolution.)

To check the size of your photo, Alt-click (Windows) or Option-click (Mac OS) the status bar at the lower left corner of the window. If one of the pixel dimensions is less than 300, you may want to rescan your photo at a higher resolution. If the photo is larger, you may want to crop it (or you can scale it down in step 8). For tips on cropping and image resizing, see "Crop and refine the photo size" on page 6.

7

Drag and drop your photos. With the postcard template window active, select the Place Photo Here layer in the Layers palette. Select the move tool, drag your photos onto the postcard image, and position them as desired.

8

Scale down the photos. If you want to make a photo smaller, select the photo's layer in the Layers palette and choose Edit > Free Transform. Shift-drag the bounding box handles to scale down the photo proportionally. Press Enter to apply the changes.

9

Hide the placeholder layer. When you're finished adding photos, click the eye icon in the Layers palette to hide the Place Photo Here layer containing the guide text.

10 **Sharpen the images.** To add more contrast and sharpness to a photo, select the photo's layer in the Layers palette and choose Filter > Sharpen > Unsharp Mask. Try using an Amount value of 100 to 150%.

11

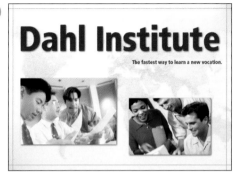

Apply the title layer effects to your photos. If desired, you can easily apply to your photos the same layer effects used for your Title type. Select the Title layer in the Layers palette, and choose Layer > Effects > Copy Effects. Then select a photo's layer and choose Layer > Effects > Paste Effects.

12

Save and print your postcard.
Choose File > Save As, rename the file, and save a working version of the postcard image. Then prepare to print the postcard:

• You can print the postcard in Photoshop format on a single-sided page. Crop marks indicate the final trim size, which is 6 by 4.25 inches.

• Or you can place the postcard image in a PageMaker template for a two-sided postcard. After you save a working layered version of the postcard, choose File > Save a Copy, rename the file, and save it in TIFF format. In PageMaker, open P09a.t65 or P09b.t65 in the Proj09 folder. On page 1, select the placeholder frame for your postcard image and choose File > Place. Accept the current settings and place the TIFF version of the postcard image. Click Yes to include the postcard image as part of the file. Complete the rest of the postcard and then print it.

For tips on card stocks to use, see "Choosing a card stock" on page 73.

Variation: Use your own photo for the postcard background

Here's a simple technique to replace the texture background of the postcard with your own photo.

Prepare the photo. In Photoshop, open the image file to be used as the new background and resize or crop it to 6.25 × 4.5 inches at a resolution of 200 ppi. This size will allow for a 1/4-inch bleed around the edges of the photo. For information on changing the size and resolution of your photo, see "Getting Your Photos Ready for Projects" on page 2.

Sharpen the image. To add more contrast and sharpen your photo after resizing, choose Filter > Sharpen > Unsharp Mask. Try using an Amount value of 100 to 150%.

3

4

Drag and drop your photo. With the postcard image window active, select the Texture layer in the Layers palette. Using the move tool, Shift-drag your photo onto the postcard image. This positions the photo in the center of the postcard. The blue guidelines indicate the trim edges of the postcard where the image will bleed. In the Layers palette, click the eye icon to hide the Texture layer.

Screen back the photo. With the new background photo layer selected, use the Opacity slider on the Layers palette to lighten the photo. Typically an opacity of 10% to 15% works well.

If you wish to view the background image without the checkerboard pattern of the grid showing through, choose File > Preferences > Transparency & Gamut, and then choose None from the Grid Size pop-up menu.

INPUT/OUTPUT: Choosing a card stock

Before you print your postcard, you'll want to talk to your printer about the different card stocks available. Although 7 points is the minimum thickness allowed for mailing a stand-alone card, 7-point stock is typically only available uncoated. Much of today's uncoated business reply mail is printed on this stock.

The ideal card stock for a postcard is 8-point stock coated on one side (commonly referred to as 8-point C1S). The advantage of coating only one side is that the image prints well on the coated glossy side while you can write on the uncoated side (for example, to fill in an appointment date and time).

Stock coated on one side comes in thicknesses of 8, 10, 12, and 14 points. Heavier stock is also available but can be too heavy to run on many presses.

Also consider the standard U.S. postal size. The maximum size for a postcard is 4.25 by 6 inches. Once you exceed that size, the postal rate increases to the cost of mailing a letter.

Tools:

Adobe Photoshop

Adobe PageMaker

Materials:

Flyer template

Your photo

Project 10

Creating a Flyer for Photocopying

Prepare a black-and-white photograph for high-quality photocopy reproduction.

 At Home Realty
10607 Culver St.
Marionville CA
95112

1930s Spanish Charmer

**1515 Dakota Ave.
Marionville CA
95111**

$298,000

Features:	• 3 Bedrooms	• Large Backyard
	• 2.5 Baths	• Screened Sunroom
	• Fireplace	• 2-Car Garage

Description: This charming house is located in a quiet neighborhood with schools, shops and restaurants nearby. Built in 1932, this structure has a solid foundation as well as fine detailing in cabinetry and molding throughout.

Contact: Ruth Everett

Phone: 555.555.5555

Email: ruth@home.com

Information provided deemed reliable but not guaranteed.

For projects that demand high volume on a tight budget, try photocopying from a laser-print master. Laser printers print images by using dots of ink called halftone cells, which vary in size to represent different levels of gray. The number of lines of halftone cells used to print each inch of the image is called the screen frequency.

Use this project to prepare a grayscale photo with appropriate halftone settings. Then place the photo in a flyer template and print the flyer on a PostScript laser printer to create a high-quality master for photocopying.

1 **Getting started.** In Photoshop, open your photo file.

Crop and resize the photo. Crop and resize the photo to a height of 3 inches or less, a width of 5 inches or less, and a resolution of 200 pixels/inch.

The flyer template can accommodate a horizontal or vertical photograph.

Convert to grayscale mode. Choose Image > Mode > Grayscale to convert the colors in the photo to levels of gray.

4 **Correct tonalities and sharpen the photo.** Choose Image > Adjust > Levels, and adjust the tonal range of the photo. Then choose Filter > Sharpen > Unsharp Mask to sharpen the photo details. For more information, see "Getting Your Photos Ready for Projects" on page 2.

5

Specify halftone settings. Choose File > Page Setup. Do one of the following to display the halftone options:

• In Windows, click the Screens button at the lower left.

• In Mac OS, click the Screen button. (You may need to choose Adobe Photoshop 5.0 from the pop-up menu first.)

Deselect Use Printer's Default Screen. Set the frequency to 65, the angle to 45, and the shape to Round.

6 **Save working and export versions of the photo.** To save a working version, choose File > Save As, rename the file, and save it in Photoshop format.

To save a version for export, choose File > Save a Copy, rename the file, and save it in Photoshop EPS format. For Preview, choose a TIFF preview; for Encoding, choose ASCII (Windows) or Binary (Mac OS). Select Include Halftone Screen.

7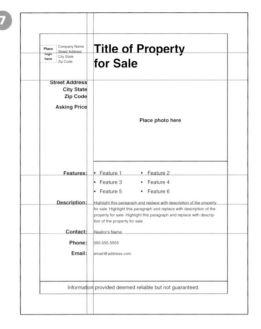

Open the flyer template. In PageMaker, open P10.t65 in the Proj10 folder.

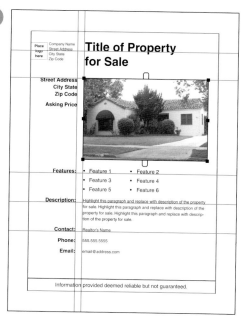

Place your photo in the flyer. Select the image frame below the title headline in the flyer, and choose File > Place. Accept the current settings and place the EPS version of the photo. Click Yes to include the photo as part of the file.

Replace the flyer text. Using the text tool (T), replace the placeholder text with your own information.

10 **Save and print the flyer.** Choose File > Save As, rename the file, and save it in PageMaker format. Then print the file on a PostScript laser printer (see "Printing a hard-copy master" on page 79).

Variation: Experiment with different halftone settings

Because printers and photocopiers vary in the precision of ink dots they can recognize and produce, you may be able to improve your flyer by trying different halftone settings in step 5. Experiment with screen frequencies between 53 (for a coarser halftone cell) and 85 (for a finer cell). You can also experiment with different shapes for the halftone cell.

For each halftone adjustment, save a separate file in EPS format, print the file, and make a test photocopy of the print. This way, you can compare the photocopy results of different halftone settings and decide on the best settings to use for your flyer. Remember that a good printed original doesn't always translate to a good photocopy!

Frequency: 30, Shape: Line

Frequency: 40, Shape: Cross

Frequency: 25, Shape: Diamond

INPUT/OUTPUT: Printing a hard-copy master

To ensure a high-quality printout with correct halftone settings, this project requires a PostScript laser printer. PostScript printers are widely available at photocopy centers with desktop publishing services.

To print your flyer at a photocopy center, copy the PageMaker file to a floppy disk. Since the flyer will be transferred to another system, you may also want to copy the files for any special fonts used in the flyer.

Tools:

Adobe Photoshop

Adobe PageMaker

Materials:

Poster templates

Stippling action

Your photo

Project 11

Creating Posters

Create eye-catching graphic backgrounds for posters.

With Photoshop, it's easy to turn your photos into bold, attention-grabbing posters. Just resize your photo and apply the provided action to create a stylized texture. Then import the result into a template for horizontal or vertical posters, and add your own text.

This project shows you how to create an 8-by-12-inch master. For information on printing a full-sized poster, see "Printing proofs and posters" on page 85.

1 **Getting started.** In Photoshop, open your photo file.

2

Crop and resize the photo. Crop and resize your photo to dimensions of 8 inches by 12 inches (for either a horizontal or vertical poster), and a resolution of 150 pixels/inch (see "Crop and refine the photo size" on page 6).

You can use a relatively low resolution for the photo because posters are generally viewed at a distance and don't require high-resolution displays of fine detail. The stippled texture you'll apply further stylizes the photo and removes the need for detail.

3

Increase photo contrast. If your photo does not contain a bold contrast between highlights and shadows, choose Image > Adjust > Brightness/ Contrast, and increase the Contrast value. Increasing the contrast improves the stippled texture effect.

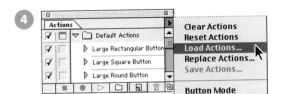

Load the stippling action. In the Actions palette, choose Load Actions from the pop-up menu and select the P11.atn file in the Proj11 folder.

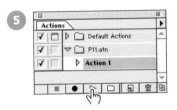

Play the Stippling action. In the Actions palette, open the P11.atn folder. Select Action 1 and click the Play button (▷) at the bottom of the palette.

In the course of playing this action, some alert messages may appear. Click OK to dismiss the messages and continue with the action.

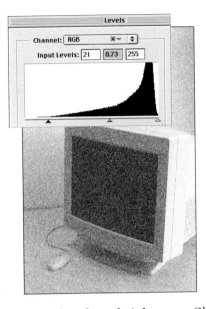

Adjust the photo brightness. Choose Image > Adjust > Levels. To darken the photo, drag the black slider under the histogram to the right. To brighten the photo, drag the white slider under the histogram to the left.

7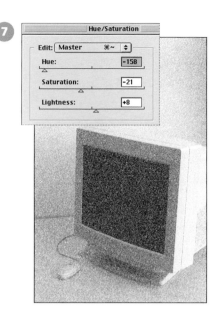

Adjust the color. Choose Image > Adjust > Hue/Saturation. To adjust the shade of color, drag the Hue slider. To adjust the strength of color, drag the Saturation slider.

8 **Save working and export versions of the photo.** To save a layered working version, choose File > Save As, rename the file, and save it in Photoshop format. To save a single-layer version for export, choose File > Save a Copy, rename the file, and save it in TIFF format.

The TIFF file is now ready to be placed in a vertical or horizontal poster template (P11a.t65 or P11b.t65 in the Proj11 folder).

Because posters are meant to capture an audience's attention, it's important to make the poster image and message bold, simple, and legible. These tips will help you create posters with immediate, universal appeal.

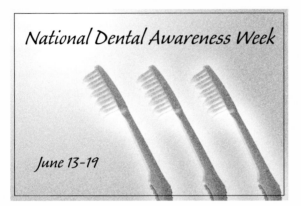

Remember that you'll be placing type over your photo! When planning the composition of your poster image, think about where you'll add the type and how much area it will occupy.

The stippling effect works well on images that have easily identifiable shapes and simple outlines. When shooting or cropping your photo, try to emphasize the subject by isolating it against a solid-colored background.

Before you print your full-sized poster, you may want to print a smaller proof version to check your design and formatting. When you're satisfied with the proof, bring the finished poster file to a service bureau that produces enlarged prints.

To print a letter-sized proof on a desktop printer:

1   In PageMaker, choose File > Print. The appearance of the Print dialog box varies with different printers, but many options are shared by most printers.

2   Set the reduction factor to 90% and print the proof file.

To print a full-sized poster:

1   In PageMaker, save the poster file in a format acceptable to your service bureau.

2   To produce a 24-by-36-inch poster, have the service bureau print the file at a 300% enlargement factor. Use different enlargement factors for other poster sizes.

Tools:

Adobe Photoshop

Materials:

Color samples

Film separation action

Your photo

Project 12

Preparing a Posterized Image for Print

Transform your photographs into colorful, print-ready posterized art.

To create dramatic posterized effects, convert a continuous-tone photograph into an image with only a few tonal levels. The resulting flat areas can be filled with different colors. The image is then ready to color separate using the supplied Photoshop action and send to your commercial screen printer.

1 **Getting started.** In Photoshop, open the photo image you want to posterize.

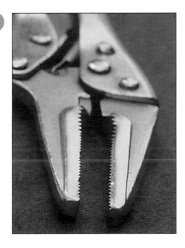

Convert to an 8-bit, grayscale image. The posterize feature requires an 8-bit image. If you are using a 16-bit image, convert it by choosing Image > Mode > 8 Bits/Channel.

Once you have an 8-bit image, choose Image > Mode > Grayscale to convert it to grayscale. In a grayscale image, each tonal level represents one color (a shade of gray), so you can set the number of colors by specifying the tonal levels.

Adjust the tonal range. To evenly distribute the levels of gray in your image before posterizing it, choose Image > Adjust > Auto Levels.

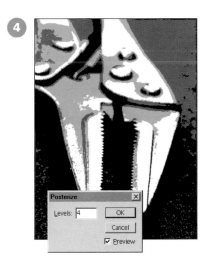

Posterize your image. Choose Image > Adjust > Posterize and enter the number of tonal levels (for example, 3 or 4). Remember that each level represents one color on your final printed piece, so using more levels will increase your prepress and printing costs.

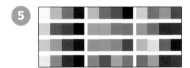

Display color samples. Open P12.psd (a file containing color samples) in the Proj12 folder. Each group of four colors is a set designed for posterized images. You can use a set to help you select ink colors for your image. Move the samples so they will be visible when you work in the image window.

Select shapes to colorize. Double-click the magic wand tool (✳), which selects areas in an image by their color.

In the Magic Wand Options palette, deselect Anti-aliased and enter 1 as the Tolerance value.

In the image, click a shape that has the lightest color and choose Select > Similar. This selects all of the shapes that are filled with the same shade of gray.

Colorize as a spot color. In the Channels palette, hold down Ctrl (Windows) or Command (Mac OS) and click the New Channel button to create a spot color channel for the selected shapes.

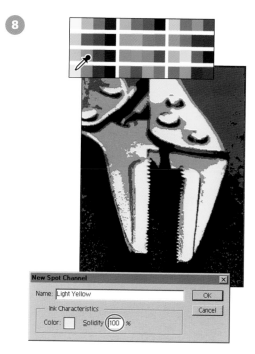

8

Picker and in the New Spot Channel dialog box. The spot channel now has the name of the specified ink color.

9

Define the color. Enter a Solidity value of **100%** to make the color preview as solid, and then click the Color box to display the Color Picker.

Move the pointer over the color samples in the file that you opened earlier. When the pointer changes to an eyedropper, select the leftmost color in a set of four colors. (You can also use the Color Picker or another method to select a color.) The selected color appears in the Color Picker.

Click Custom to select a matching color from a color system (by default, this is a PANTONE color system for printing inks). The Custom Colors dialog box displays the color closest to the selected color in the Color Picker. Click OK and then confirm your selection in the Color

Colorize the rest of the image. In the Channels palette, click the channel that represents your original image. By default, this is the Black channel. Select this channel and repeat steps 6 through 8 for each of the gray levels in your image. Colorize the lighter levels first and continue until the entire image is colorized. If you are using one of the color sets provided, work from left to right through a set, so that the rightmost color replaces the darkest shade of gray.

To save a working version of your file before you prepare it for film output, choose File > Save As, rename the file, and save it in Photoshop format.

Separate for film. In the Actions palette, choose Load Actions from the palette menu. Select P12.atn (a file containing a set of actions to automate film separation) in the Proj12 folder.

Select the Create Separations action and click the Play button. When prompted, click Continue and then name the file that will contain the separations (for example, use the filename of your working file and add the extension .sep). The new file will contain only the spot color channels. After you name the file, the action runs without interruption.

Variation: Prepare an image for an inkjet printer

If you are not going to color-separate your image, you don't have to apply custom colors to individual spot channels. Instead, you can apply color directly to the image. Most of the preparation steps are the same.

1 Convert to a color image. After posterizing the grayscale image (step 4), convert it to RGB mode by choosing Image > Mode > RGB Color.

2 Select a color. After selecting the shapes with the lightest tonal level (step 6), use one of these methods to select a color to fill the shapes:

- Select the eyedropper tool (⌀) and then select the leftmost color in one of the sets in the color sample file (step 5).

- In the Color palette, select a color from the color bar.

- In the Swatches palette, select a color swatch.

- Click on the foreground color swatch in the toolbox and then use the Color Picker.

3 Colorize the image shapes. Choose Edit > Fill to apply the color to the selected shapes. Select Foreground Color and Normal mode, and enter **100%** as the Opacity value.

4 Colorize the rest of the image. Apply different colors to each of the gray levels in your image, colorizing the lighter levels first, until the entire image is colorized. If you are using one of the color sets provided, work from left to right through the set, so that the rightmost color replaces the darkest shade of gray.

5 Save and print the image. Choose File > Save As, rename and save the file, and then print the image. Do not use the color-separation action described in step 10.

Depending on the subject matter, you may be able to use Sharpen or Blur filters to enhance a posterized image before you create color separations. You can help keep the image recognizable—even with an adventuresome choice of hues—by matching the brightness of the gray levels you replace.

If you need to scale a posterized image, choose Image > Image Size and set the Resample Image option to Nearest Neighbor. This helps to maintain distinct edges between the solid shapes.

Human figures usually look better with less detail and softer, smoother shapes. Try applying one of the Blur filters, such as Gaussian Blur.

Industrial subjects usually look better with crisper shapes and more detail. Try applying one of the Sharpen filters, such as Unsharp Mask.

When you add color to a posterized image, replace each level of gray with a color that has a similar luminosity value (brightness). Replace light grays with light colors and dark grays with dark colors.

Tools:

Adobe Photoshop

Materials:

Adjust and save actions

Image border actions

Your photos

Project 13

Batch-Processing Images for Print

Make print production and border treatments easier by batch-processing your images.

Batch processing in Photoshop lets you apply color corrections, edits, or special effects to a series of images by playing the same action on all files and subfolders in a folder. This time-saving technique replicates in minutes the editing that would take much longer if you opened and adjusted each image individually. For example, you could batch-process a series of catalog images, all requiring the same dimensions, color, border treatment, and file format.

1 **Getting started.** From the desktop, organize the files that you'll batch-process by placing them into one folder (the source folder). To preserve the original images, create a folder into which you'll save the batch-processed files (the destination folder).

For best printed results, the images should have a resolution of 300 pixels per inch. (However, if the final image dimensions will be larger than 5 inches by 7 inches, you may want to reduce the resolution to keep the file size manageable.) In Photoshop, crop and resize your images if necessary, before starting the batch process (see "Crop and refine the photo size" on page 6).

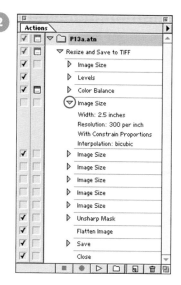

Load your action. In the Actions palette, choose Load Actions from the palette menu and select the P13a.atn file in the Proj13 folder. The Resize and Save to TIFF action appears in the P13a.atn folder in the Actions palette. This action sharpens and adjusts the image contrast automatically, and lets you choose an image size before you save the images as TIFF (a file format commonly used in print production).

Click the triangle next to a command (such as Image Size) to see the settings made by the command. You can adjust the settings as needed for specific corrections—for example, to adjust a specific color cast, levels, or contrast.

Adjust the color correction and contrast levels. Open an image in the batch of images you plan to adjust. In the Actions palette, double-click the Color Balance command in the Resize and Save to TIFF action. Make sure that Preview is selected and the image window is visible. Select Shadows and move the sliders to adjust the color balance. Repeat for the image's midtones and highlights until the image's color looks correct.

Now when you run your batch process, all of your images will have that color correction done automatically. When you have finished adjusting the command, close the image without saving it.

Choose an image size. The first Image Size command in the action sets the resolution to 300 pixels per inch and sets the size of the original image. Select a different Image Size command if you want to change the size of the images by clicking in the leftmost column next to the command. (Or you can double-click an Image Size command and edit it to suit your own project.)

A check mark indicates that a command is included in the action and will be applied to a batch of images. A dialog box icon indicates a modal control that pauses an action until you press Enter; to avoid a pause, click the icon to hide it and turn off the modal control.

⑤

Batch-process your images. Choose File > Automate > Batch. For Set, choose P13a.atn. For Action, choose Resize and Save to TIFF. For Source, click Choose and select the folder of images you organized in step 1. For Destination, click Choose and select the folder you created in step 1 for the processed and saved files. If you don't want the Save As dialog box to appear each time a file is saved, select the Override Action "Save In" Commands option. Click OK to run the batch process.

Variation: Try other actions for different border effects

Once you have batch-processed your images for color corrections and image size, you can add a border effect to the processed images.

❶

Add a border to your images. Open one of the processed images to use as a test. From the Actions palette menu, choose Load Actions and select the file named P13b.atn in the Proj13 folder. A set of actions for different border effects appears in your palette.

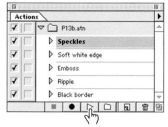

Experiment with different borders.
In the Actions palette, select an action (such as Speckles) and click the Play button (▷) to apply the effect to your test image. If you don't like the effect, show the History palette and select the original version of the image at the top of the palette. Then select and play a different action in the Actions palette.

❸ Apply the border effects to your batch. If you like the result and want to apply it to the rest of your images, close your image without saving it. Organize into one source folder all images to which you'll apply the border effects, and create another destination folder for the processed and saved images. Then run the batch process using the selected action to apply the border effect to the images.

Speckles

Soft white edge

Emboss

Ripple

Black border

When applying the same adjustments to a batch of images, you can organize your images by common flaws that the originals share—for example, a color cast introduced by a scanner, graininess, or too much or too little contrast. Or you can organize the images according to their final treatment—uniform dimensions or the same border treatment.

Before processing, these photographs have an undesirable color cast.

After processing, the color cast has been removed and a border has been added.

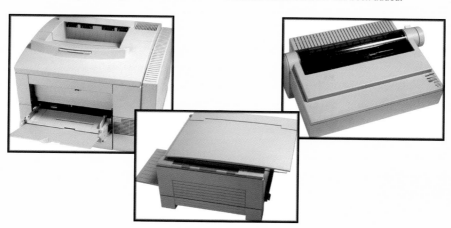

Tools:

Adobe ImageReady

Materials:

Resize and save droplets

Image border actions

Your photos

Project 14

Batch-Processing Images for the Web

Make Web production and border treatments easier by batch-processing your images.

Batch processing in ImageReady lets you apply color corrections, edits, or special effects to a series of images and save them in a Web format by dragging a folder to a droplet. This time-saving technique replicates the editing that would take much longer if you opened and adjusted each image individually. For example, if you have 20 images to save as JPEG files, you can use batch processing to perform this task in minutes.

① **Getting started.** Organize the files that you'll batch-process by placing them in a source folder. For tips on how to organize them, see "Organizing a batch of images" on page 97.

If any of your images require cropping, crop them before starting the batch process. For best results, the final images for the Web should be 72 ppi. Because the images you open in ImageReady are always 72 ppi, all you have to do is select the pixel size of your final image when you set up the batch process.

②

Open a droplet. In ImageReady, open either the P14a.exe file (the droplet to save as GIF) or the P14b.exe file (the droplet to save as JPEG) in the Proj14 folder.

Each droplet automatically sharpens and adjusts your images' contrast, lets you choose the image dimensions, and saves the images in GIF or JPEG format for Web production (see "Appendix: Choosing a File Format" on page 177).

③

Select the image size. Click the triangles next to the Resize Image commands to show the final image size (in pixels) that each command will produce. When you find the desired image size, click the leftmost column next to it—the check mark indicates your selection. Only selected commands will be applied to a batch of images.

4

Batch-process your images for the Web. Choose File > Save As, rename the file to indicate the image size (for future reference), and save your droplet to the desktop. Drag the folder of images that you want to batch-process onto the droplet. ImageReady saves the images in the same ("Source") folder, but appends the .gif or .jpg extension, depending on which droplet you opened in step 2.

Variation: Try other actions for different border effects

Once you have batch-processed images for their size and Web format, you can add a border effect to them using one of the provided actions. Before you can use the Crosshatch or Ripple effects, you need a copy of the Photoshop plug-in in your ImageReady Plug-ins folder.

1 **Add a border to your images.** Quit ImageReady and open the Borders folder in the Proj14 folder. Select the

folder's contents and place them in the Actions folder in the ImageReady folder. Then restart ImageReady.

You must restart ImageReady to make the actions available in the Actions palette.

2

Run a test. In ImageReady, open a processed Web image to test the border effects. In the Actions palette, select one of the Border actions and click the Play button (▷) to apply the effect to your image.

The Texturize_burlap effect requires a preselected foreground color before playing the action. To use the Crosshatch or Ripple effect, copy the corresponding Photoshop plug-in from the Photoshop Plug-ins Effects or Filters folders into the ImageReady Plug-ins folder.

P14c.isa—
Texturize_burlap

P14d.isa—
Foreground color

P14e.isa—Soft Edge

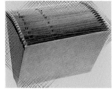

P14f.isa—Crosshatch

P14g.isa—Ripple

3 **Experiment with different effects.**
If you don't like the result, choose
Edit > Undo to return to the original
image. Then run other border effects
as desired.

4

Create a droplet for batch processing.
If you like the result and want to apply
the effect to the rest of your images, you
can create a droplet. In the Actions
palette, select the border action and
then choose Batch Options from the
palette menu.

In the Batch Options dialog box, select
Optimized and choose Specific Folder
from the pop-up menu. Click Choose
and then either select a destination
folder or create a new one. Click OK to
close the Batch Options dialog box.
In the Actions palette, choose Create
Droplet from the palette menu. Save
the droplet to the desktop.

You can now apply the border effect
globally by dragging your folder of
images onto the droplet. (The border
effect is applied to all the images in the
folder regardless of their file formats.)

Project 15

Creating Binder Covers

Add flair to your binder covers by filling titles or other shapes with images.

With Photoshop, it's easy to display an image within any shape, including the shape of type. You create the shape on one layer, add the image to an adjacent layer, and then group the layers. You can use this image-clipping technique to create a title for a binder cover, and then place the title in a PageMaker template.

① **Getting started.** In Photoshop, open P15a.psd (a template for the cover title) in the Proj15 folder.

②

Type your title. In the Layers palette, double-click the Cover Title layer to open the Type Tool dialog box. To preview how the new title will fit in the image window, make sure that Preview is selected and that you can see both the dialog box and the image window. Then select the text in the dialog box and replace it with your title.

If you wish, change the font and adjust the size and leading. Make sure the whole title appears in the image window, which is the same size as the title area in the binder cover template. If the title does not fit, adjust the font size as needed.

③

Add an image. Open the file that contains the image you want to appear in the title. (For best results, use an image that is 5.5 inches wide by 2.3 inches high, or larger, with a resolution of 150 pixels per inch or higher.) Then choose Select > All and Edit > Copy. Make the template window active and choose Edit > Paste. This copies the image to a new layer in the template.

Group the layers. With the new layer still selected, choose Layer > Group with Previous. This creates a clipping group that includes the type layer and the layer containing the image. The image appears within the outline of the type.

You could achieve the same effect by using the type mask tool (T), but the resulting text could not be edited. Text in a type layer of a clipping group can still be edited.

5 **Save working and export versions of the file.** To save a layered working version, choose File > Save As, rename the file, and save it in Photoshop format. To save a single-layer version for export to PageMaker, choose File > Save a Copy, rename the file, and save it in TIFF format.

6 **Open a PageMaker template.** In PageMaker, open P15a.t65 (the template for the front cover of the binder) in the Proj15 folder.

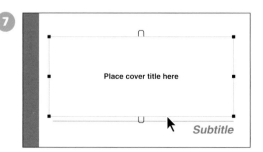

Place the image. Select the large frame provided for the cover title, and choose File > Place. Accept the current settings and place the TIFF version of the cover title. Click Yes to include the image as part of the file.

8 **Edit the front cover.** Place a logo or other graphic in the small frame at the lower left and replace the other text on the page with the text for your project. If you wish, adjust the font, size, and color of the text and change the colors of other items on the page. Then choose File > Save As and rename and save the file.

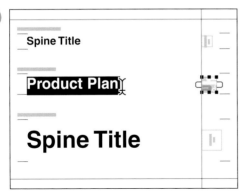

Create the spine cover. Open
P15b.t65 (the template for the spine
cover) in the Proj15 folder. The
template provides spine covers of
different widths. Edit the spine cover
that fits your binder by replacing the
text with your cover title and placing a
logo or other graphic in the frame to the
right. Then choose File > Save As and
rename and save the file.

Assemble the binder cover. Print the
files for the front cover and spine cover.
Cut out the spine cover and slide the
front cover sheet and the spine sheet
into the binder.

Variation: Placing images in shadow boxes

To achieve other special effects, clip
your images within shapes. For
example, to create a binder cover that
appears to have snapshots scattered on
its surface, display several photo
images within shadow boxes.

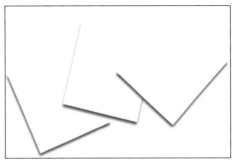

Copy images to a template. In
Photoshop, open P15b.psd in the
Proj15 folder. This template file has
three layers, each containing a
rectangle with a drop shadow. Copy
three photo files to the template (the
images should be 3 by 3 inches or
larger, with a resolution of 150 pixels
per inch). Each photo image is copied
to a new layer.

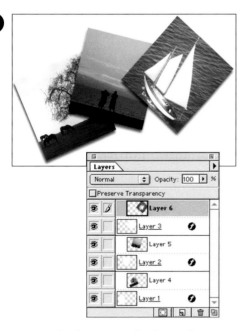

2

Select each photo layer and choose Edit > Transform > Rotate. Drag each image until its rotation matches that of the shadow box it occupies, and press Enter when you're finished. If necessary, use the move tool (⊹) to reposition the image within the shadow box. When all the images are in place, rename and save the file and then save a copy in TIFF format.

3 Create the binder cover. In PageMaker, open the P15c.t65 template file in the Proj15 folder. Place your TIFF file in the large frame provided and then edit the text and make any other desired changes to the front cover page. Use the P15b.t65 template to create the spine cover.

Group the layers and adjust the images. Arrange the layers so that each photo is above the shadow box it will occupy. Then select each photo layer and choose Layer > Group with Previous. The images appear within their shadow boxes.

Displaying an image within the type can help showcase your binder's title. Here are some tips for choosing a typeface and background image to use for a bold, legible title.

Background image

Avoid narrow typefaces.

Use a large, bold or extra-bold typeface so that the title stands out and more of the image shows through.

Background image

Background image

Using objects for the background creates ambiguous shapes showing through the type and makes it hard to read the title.

Using textures or patterns for the background image creates a title that's simple and easy to read.

Tools:

Adobe Photoshop

Adobe PageMaker

Materials:

CD cover template

Your image files

Project 16

Creating a Contact Sheet for a CD Cover

Use a contact sheet to catalog thumbnail images and display them on the cover of your CD.

Cataloging your image files on contact sheets can help you keep track of the images stored on a compact disc. Place the contact sheet images on the pages of a CD cover booklet designed to slip inside the front of the jewel case.

The PageMaker template for the CD cover includes a jewel case booklet and a single-sided back panel. The booklet contains four double-sided pages and folds in half to create eight sides.

1 **Getting started.** Assemble all of your image files in one source folder. Organize them alphabetically by name.

2 **Specify contact sheet dimensions.** In Photoshop, choose File > Automate > Contact Sheet. Specify a width of 4.75 inches, a height of 4.75 inches, and a resolution of 150 pixels per inch or greater, depending on the printer's resolution.

3

Specify the number and order of thumbnail images. Photoshop arranges the thumbnail images in alphabetical order in rows and columns on the contact sheet. In the Contact Sheet dialog box, select Place Across First to arrange the images from left to right or select Place Down First to arrange them from top to bottom. To fit 25 thumbnail images on a sheet, specify 5 columns and 5 rows.

CDs can hold approximately one hundred 300 ppi images. At 25 thumbnail images per contact sheet, the CD cover template can easily hold 100 thumbnail images on four sides of the booklet, with four sides to spare for descriptive text.

④ Select the images folder and automate. In the Contact Sheet dialog box, click Choose Source Folder and select the folder that contains your images. Click OK to automate the contact sheets. Photoshop creates a separate untitled contact sheet for every 25 image files.

⑤ Save working and export versions of the contact sheets. To save a layered working version, choose File > Save and save each contact sheet in Photoshop format. To save a single-layer version for export to PageMaker, choose File > Save a Copy, and save the files in TIFF format.

⑥

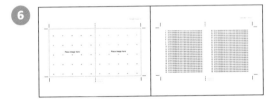

Open the CD cover template. In PageMaker, open the P16a.t65 file in the Proj16 folder, choose File > Save As, and save it with a different name.

⑦

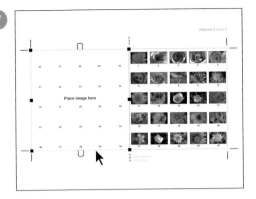

Place contact sheets. Select the place-holder frame on the right side of the first page in the template and choose File > Place. Accept the current settings and place the first contact sheet. (Click Yes to include the contact sheet image as part of the CD cover file.) This will be the front of the CD cover booklet.

If you have more than one contact sheet, repeat this step to place the other contact sheets where you want them in the booklet.

If necessary, move the text numbers below the images or delete them.

8 **Fill in the descriptive text.** Select the type tool (**T**), highlight the various text blocks, and replace them with your own text. If the text blocks are not appropriate, delete them. If you wish, move the text around or format it using the Styles palette.

9 **Save and print the CD cover.** Delete any pages that you didn't use, and save the changes. The booklet is designed to be printed on double-sided pages. The last page of the template is designed to be printed on one side for the back panel of the jewel case.

Choose File > Print. If you're using a printer that prints double-sided pages, choose Both Pages from the Print pop-up menu and print the file. If you need to manually turn over the paper to print the other side of each page, choose Odd Pages from the Print pop-up menu and print the odd pages first. Set aside the last printed page for the back panel. Then place the printed odd pages of the booklet upside down in the printer, choose File > Print, and print the even pages.

10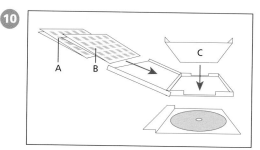

A. Outside cover 1   B. Outside cover 2
C. Back panel

Assemble the CD cover. Assemble the pages of the booklet, trim along the gray dashed lines, and fold along the gray dotted lines. Slip the folded pages of the booklet into the front of the CD jewel case. Trim along the gray dashed lines on the page for the back panel. Remove the plastic insert that holds the CD within the jewel case, and place the back panel so that the descriptive text (name, address, date, and spine title) is visible from the outside. Snap the CD insert back into place and you've completed your project.

Tools:

Adobe Photoshop

Adobe PageMaker

Materials:

CD cover template

Your photos

Project 17

Blending Images for a CD Cover

Use blended images and a semitransparent title backdrop for creative CD packaging.

Here is a technique that blends two images together for an interesting effect that you can use on the cover of a compact disc. To complete the effect, create a title with a semitransparent backdrop.

The PageMaker template for the CD cover includes a jewel case booklet and back panel. The booklet is a double-sided page that folds in half to create four sides. The back panel is a single-sided page designed to fit in the back of the jewel case.

① **Getting started.** In Photoshop, open two image files to use as the background and foreground of the blended image.

②

Make both images the same size. Resize and/or crop both images to be 4.875 inches wide, 5 inches high, and a resolution of at least 150 pixels per inch. Make sure the resolution is the same for both images. For tips on image resizing and resolution, see "Crop and refine the photo size" on page 6.

The combined images will bleed .125 inch beyond the CD cover boundary on three sides (the fourth side is on the fold). Once placed in the PageMaker template, printed, and trimmed, the image will be 4.75 by 4.75 inches square.

③

Paste one image on top of the other. Choose Select > All to select everything in the foreground image window and then choose Edit > Copy. Close the file.

With the background image window active, choose Edit > Paste. This pastes the foreground image on a separate layer in the background image file.

④ **Save the new combined file.** Choose File > Save As and save the combined file with a different name in Photoshop format. This will be your working file, to use whenever you need to edit individual layers (such as type layers).

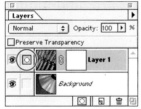

Create a layer mask. With the top layer selected, choose Layer > Add Layer Mask > Reveal All to add a mask to the foreground image.

In the Layers palette, a white thumbnail image of the new mask appears on the layer, next to a link icon (⅜) that indicates the mask is linked to the layer. The paintbrush icon changes to a white circle, indicating the mask is selected for editing.

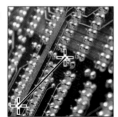
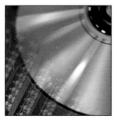

Blend the two images together. With the mask selected, select the gradient tool (▦) and drag it across the foreground image. (The white thumbnail image of the mask in the Layers palette changes to a grayscale gradient.)

If you are not satisfied with the result, drag the gradient tool in a different area or direction or with a shorter or longer line. You can always use the History palette to return to your favorite version.

Create the title. Select the type tool (T) and click inside the blended image. This creates a new, editable text layer and displays the Type Tool dialog box.

Select the Preview option and then type the title of the CD. Select the title and choose a font, font size, and color.

8

Create a semitransparent container for the title. In the Layers palette, select the foreground image layer, choose New Layer from the pop-up menu and name the new layer for the container. The new layer should be below the title layer.

Select the rectangular marquee tool (⬚) and drag it to draw a rectangle for the container behind the CD cover's title. If you prefer rounded corners on the rectangle, choose Select > Feather and enter the number of pixels for the Feather Radius (for example, 4 pixels).

To fill the container, choose Edit > Fill. For Contents, choose White and make sure that Opacity is set to 100% and Mode is set to Normal.

With the container layer selected, use the Opacity slider at the top of the Layers palette to enter a percentage for the opacity of the selected layer (such as 20%). Choose Select > Deselect to deselect the rectangle.

9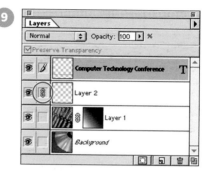

Link the title to its backdrop. In the Layers palette, select the title layer and then click in the box to the left of the container layer name. A link icon appears, indicating that the layer is linked. With the title layer selected, use the move tool (▶﹢) to reposition the title and the container together.

10 **Save working and export versions of the image.** Save the working file, and then choose File > Save a Copy, rename the file, and save it in TIFF format.

11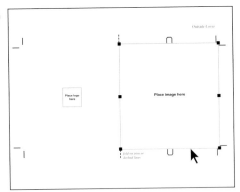

13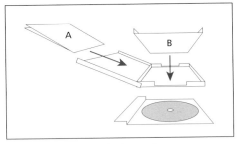

A. Outside cover   B. Back panel

Place the image in a template.
In PageMaker, open P17.t65 (the template for the CD cover) in the Proj17 folder. On the right side of the first page, select the placeholder frame for the cover image and choose File > Place. Accept the current settings and place the TIFF version of the image file. (Click Yes to include the image as part of the CD cover file.) This will be the front side of the CD cover booklet.

Assemble the CD cover. When you're finished, save and print the CD cover. To assemble the cover as a folded four-sided booklet for the front panel of a jewel case and a page for the back panel, trim along the gray dashed lines and fold along the gray dotted lines. Slip the folded booklet into the front of the CD jewel case. Remove the plastic insert that holds the CD within the jewel case, place the back panel so that the descriptive text is visible from the outside, and snap the CD insert back into place.

12 **Complete the descriptive text.** Select the type tool (**T**), highlight the various text blocks, and replace them with your own text. If the text blocks are not appropriate, delete them. If you wish, move the text around or format it using the Styles palette.

Generally, combining a bold image with a complex or patterned image (that doesn't have a focal point) improves the likelihood of a successful blend. The treatment of the title block and the type of gradient used to blend images can greatly impact your final composition as well.

A tight title block with extreme feathering can add dramatic impact to a composition.

A radial gradient maintains the harmonious tone of the artwork. The oval title block complements the organic imagery.

The clean rectangular edge and minimal feathering of this title block are in sync with the CD's topic.

Tools:

Adobe Photoshop

Adobe PageMaker

Materials:

Photo template

Video cover template

Your photo

Project 18

Creating Videotape Covers

Use a diffusion dither effect to create grainy, filmlike images for your videotape covers.

You can create a grainy, filmlike effect for the front cover image on your videotape by converting the image to Bitmap mode using the Diffusion Dither method. Here's a technique for creating two images in custom picture frames for the front and spine of a videotape cover. A PageMaker template is provided for the videotape cover and is designed to fit in a clear plastic video case.

① **Getting started.** In Photoshop, open the color photo you'll use for the front cover. Crop and resize the photo to a height of 2.6 inches, a width of 2.6 inches, and a resolution of 72 pixels per inch. For information on resizing images, see "Crop and refine the photo size" on page 6.

For this technique, your image must be in RGB color mode. If necessary, choose Image > Mode > RGB Color to convert it.

②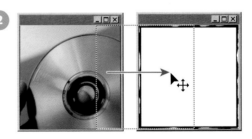

Place the image in the front cover picture frame. Open the P18.psd file (the custom picture frame template) in the Proj18 folder. This template contains a background layer and two picture frame layers to use on the front and spine of the videotape cover.

In the Layers palette, select the Background layer. Arrange the image windows so you can see both the picture frame template and your photo.

Select the move tool (▸₊) and Shift-drag the photo onto the template, releasing the mouse when the template window becomes highlighted. Photoshop creates a new layer in the template file, with the photo between the Background and the Spine layer.

3 **Flatten the layers.** Make sure that the Spine layer is hidden (if necessary, click the eye icon to hide it) and that the Cover layer for the front cover picture frame is showing. Choose Layer > Flatten Image and click OK to discard the hidden layer.

5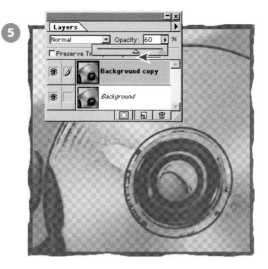

4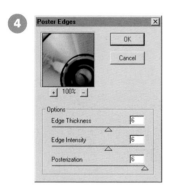

Posterize the photo. Choose Filter > Artistic > Poster Edges and experiment with different values for the posterized effect.

Convert to grayscale and adjust the opacity. Choose Image > Mode > Grayscale to convert the image from RGB to Grayscale mode. Because the layers were flattened in step 3, you'll need to create a new background layer so you can adjust its opacity. In the Layers palette, drag the Background layer to the New Layer button at the bottom of the palette. With the Background copy layer selected, drag the Opacity slider to 60% to increase the transparency of the image. Then select the original Background layer and delete it.

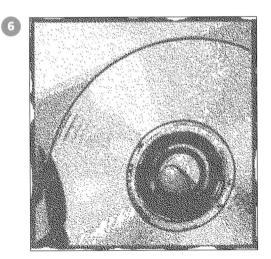

6

Convert the image to Bitmap mode.
Create a grainy, filmlike effect by
converting the image to Bitmap mode
using the Diffusion Dither method.
Choose Image > Mode > Bitmap and
click OK to flatten the image. In the
Bitmap dialog box, enter an Output
Resolution of **72** pixels/inch and select
Diffusion Dither.

7 **Save the front cover image.** Choose
File > Save As, rename the file, and save
the front cover image in TIFF format.

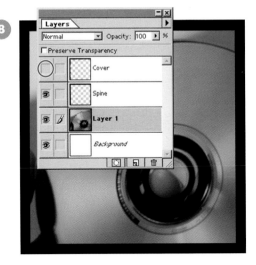

8

**Prepare the image for the spine
cover.** Reopen the picture frame
template P18.psd in the Proj18 folder.
In the Layers palette, click the eye icon
in the leftmost column next to the
Cover layer to hide the layer and then
click in the leftmost column next to the
Spine layer to show that layer.

Use the color photo you opened in
step 1 (or open another image). Select
the move tool and Shift-drag the photo
onto the template. In the Layers
palette, make sure that the new layer is
between the Spine layer and the
Background layer, the Spine layer is
showing, and the Cover layer is hidden.
Choose Layer > Flatten Image and
click OK to discard the hidden layer.

9 **Save the spine cover image.** Choose File > Save As, rename the file, and save the image for the spine of the videotape cover in TIFF format.

10

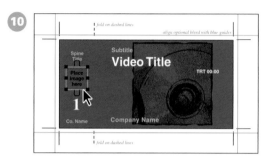

Place the images in the videotape cover template. In PageMaker, open the file P18.t65 in the Proj18 folder. Select the large placeholder frame on the cover and choose File > Place. Accept the current settings and place the TIFF version of the front cover image that you saved in step 7. Repeat this step to place the TIFF version of the spine cover image.

11

Customize the text. In PageMaker, use the type tool (T) to select the placeholder text and replace it with your own text. You can change the font, size, and color of the text using the Styles palette.

12

Save and print the videotape cover. Choose File > Save and rename the file to suit your project. Print the cover, trim along the crop marks, fold, and slip the cover into the video case.

A custom cover gives your videotapes a polished look. Here are some tips to consider when you modify the supplied template or design a cover from scratch.

The background should contrast with the type in color and texture. Darker background colors work better with reverse type.

Set up a bleed for the background if you plan to have a commercial printer produce covers in large quantities.

Materials:

Mask templates

Ad template

Your photo

Project 19

Creating an Ad for the Yellow Pages

Create a soft-edged grayscale image for use in a telephone directory ad.

With Photoshop and PageMaker, you can quickly create advertisements to be placed in a classified directory such as the Yellow Pages. Use your own photo in conjunction with a mask template to create a soft-edged effect; then place the result into the ad template for final sizing and headline copy.

1 **Getting started.** In Photoshop, open your photo file.

Convert the photo to grayscale mode. Choose Image > Mode > Grayscale and then click OK.

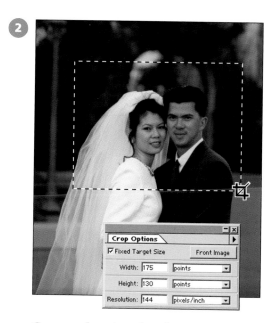

Crop and resize the photo. Crop and resize the photo to a height of 130 points, a width of 175 points, and a resolution of 144 pixels/inch (see "Crop and refine the photo size" on page 6).

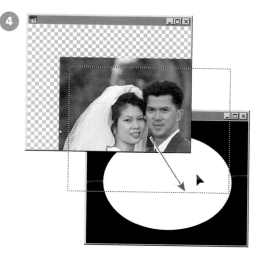

Drag and drop your photo onto a mask template. Open a mask template in the Proj19 folder. (Use P19a.psd for an oval photo, or P19b.psd for a rectangular photo.) Arrange the image windows so that you can see both your photo and the mask template.

Select the move tool (⊹) and Shift-drag your photo into the mask template, releasing the mouse when the template window becomes highlighted. Your photo is copied and centered in the template. Make sure that the template window is active.

Select the mask shape. In the Layers palette, Ctrl-click (Windows) or Command-click (Mac OS) the Oval or Rectangle layer to select the mask shape.

Subtract the mask shape from the photo. Select your photo layer in the Layers palette. Then choose Select > Feather, enter **8**, and click OK. Feathering gives a softer edge to the selection outline.

Now press Backspace (Windows) or Delete (Mac OS) to remove the mask area from the photo. In the Layers palette, hide the Oval or Rectangle layer.

7 **Save working and export versions of the template file.** To save a layered working version, choose File > Save As, rename the file, and save it in Photoshop format. To save a single-layer version for export, choose File > Save a Copy, rename the file, and save it in TIFF format.

The TIFF version of the file is ready for placement in the ad template.

8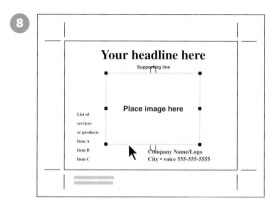

Open the ad template. In Adobe PageMaker, open P19.t65 in the Proj19 folder. This file contains page layouts for three different ad sizes.

9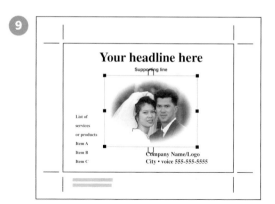

Place your photo in the ad template. Select the desired image frame in the template, and choose File > Place. Accept the current settings and place the TIFF version of your photo. Click Yes to include the photo as part of the file.

10

Customize the ad copy. Using the text tool (T), replace the sample text with your own copy. Save and print the ad file.

Think about how you can make your ad stand out from other ads on the same directory page. Does the ad appeal to your target customers? Is your ad image communicative or striking enough? The following tips can help you boost the effectiveness of your ad.

Use brief headlines to capture the attention of your customers and communicate a clear, direct message.

White space can add to the impact of your piece.

Use different fonts to highlight important points, such as your business name or location.

Try not to crowd your ad with a photo containing busy elements.

Tools:

Adobe Photoshop

Adobe PageMaker

Materials:

Background template

Page layout template

Your image or logo

Project 20

Creating Name Tags

Create name tags for an event using these simple techniques and templates.

Using the two templates supplied for this project, it's easy to create name tags for your special event. Here is a technique to create a sheet of name tags that can be trimmed and inserted into plastic slipcovers. Customize the design and add your logo to the name tag template. Then use the PageMaker template to produce the sheet of name tags, add individual names to each tag, and print it on a laser or inkjet printer.

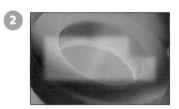

Getting started. In Photoshop, open the P20.psd file (the name tag template) in the Proj20 folder. This template contains several background images, a logo, and placeholder text for an event title. Each is on its own layer and can be edited or replaced with your own images, logo, and title.

Choose a background. Starting at the top of the Layers palette, click the eye icons to hide the Background layers you don't want to use.

If you wish to add your own background image to the template, first crop or resize it to be 3.75 inches wide, 2.4 inches high, and 200 pixels per inch for the resolution. For information on image resizing, see "Crop and refine the photo size" on page 6.

Make the name tag template window active and select the Background 1 layer. Arrange the windows so you can see both the name tag template and your new background image, and select the move tool (⤧). Shift-drag your new background image into the name tag template, releasing the mouse when the template window becomes highlighted. Your background image is centered and copied onto a new layer in the template.

Add your event title. In the Layers palette, double-click the Name of Company/Event layer to open the Type Tool dialog box. Select the text and replace it with your own event title. Change the font, size, and style as desired. You'll want some contrast between the event title and the individuals' names that will be added later in PageMaker.

Make sure to keep the text inside the blue guidelines, which indicate the trim margins for the name tag. (Choose View > Show Guides if they're not visible.)

Change the color and opacity of the event title. In the Layers palette, select the type layer. You'll change the type layer's color and opacity so that it stands out well against the background image. Select a foreground color that contrasts well with your background and then press Alt+Backspace (Windows) or Option+Delete (Mac OS) to apply the color to the type. If desired, use the Opacity slider

to adjust the transparency of the type. To make the text completely opaque, drag the slider to 100%.

Add your own logo. In the Layers palette, click the eye icon to hide the existing Logo layer. If your logo is saved in a vector art file format such as Illustrator EPS, choose File > Place and select your logo. Resize the logo as needed by Shift-dragging a corner handle and position it in the layout. Double-click the logo to rasterize and place it.

If your logo is in a bitmap format, for example, a Photoshop image, you can copy and paste or drag and drop the logo onto the template file. Then, use the Free Transform command to resize it and press Enter.

If your logo contains solid areas of color, you can make them transparent to reveal the image underneath. Double-click the magic wand tool (✱) and set the Tolerance to 32 pixels with Anti-aliased selected in the Magic Wand Options palette. Click to select the solid areas, and then delete them. When you're done, choose Select > Deselect All to deselect the image.

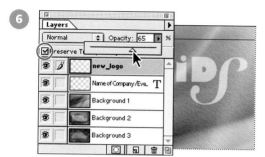

Paint the logo. To make the logo white and partially transparent so that it contrasts with a background, make the Logo layer active in the Layers palette and select the Preserve Transparency option. In the Swatches palette, select white for the foreground color. Press Alt+Backspace (Windows) or Option+Delete (Mac OS) to fill the layer with white. In the Layers palette, drag the Opacity slider to a value you like (65% in this example).

Save working and export versions of the name tag file. To save a layered version of the artwork, choose File > Save As, rename the file, and save it in Photoshop format. To save a single-layer version for export to PageMaker, choose File > Save a Copy, rename the file, and save it in TIFF format.

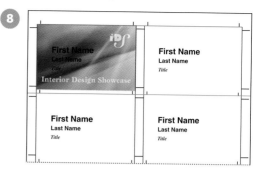

Place the name tag image. In PageMaker, open the template P20.t65 in the Proj20 folder. Select the frame in the top left corner of the page and choose File > Place. Accept the current settings and select the TIFF version of your name tag image. Click Yes to include the name tag image as part of the file.

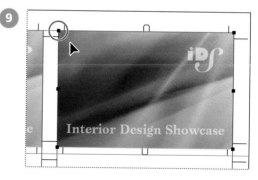

Create a set of name tags. The template can hold eight name tags on the page. With the name tag image selected, choose Edit > Copy and then choose Edit > Paste seven times to create the other name tags. Use the guidelines to position the copies between the trim marks on the page.

When you have positioned all the copies, Shift-click to select them and choose Element > Arrange > Send to Back.

Type in participant names. Use the type tool (**T**) to select the placeholder text and replace it with the names and titles you want on the name tags. You can change the font, size, and color of the text using the Styles palette.

Print name tags and trim. Choose File > Print to print the page of name tags. Cut along the trim marks and insert each name tag into a plastic slipcover. Once trimmed, the name tag is 3-1/2 by 2-1/6 inches to fit a standard plastic name tag slipcover with a metal clip.

Variation: Create name tags with space for handwritten names

Another option, especially for a large crowd or unconfirmed guest list, is to print the name tags without the participants' names and titles on them. Guests can write in their own names when they attend the event.

Prepare the file for unprinted names. Before placing the name tag image in step 8, select all the text boxes in the PageMaker template and either delete them or choose Element > Non-Printing. Then place the name tag image and make copies of it as described in steps 8 and 9.

Print and trim the name tags. Print the page, cut along the trim marks, and write in the participant names by hand.

INPUT/OUTPUT: Tips for low-resolution printing

This project assumes that you are printing to a 600 dpi, or better, color laser or inkjet printer. The lower your printer resolution, the less detail you'll want to include in your artwork.

Here are a few tips for low-resolution printing:

○ Keep background textures light in color and simple in design so that they don't distract from type legibility. Lightening and blurring images in Photoshop is a good technique. Adding a drop shadow behind type can also help to set it off.

○ Avoid using high-contrast textures behind the text because they decrease legibility.

○ Keep type treatments bold, simple, and easy to read from a distance. Avoid italics and try to use type sizes no smaller than 14 to 16 points.

Tools:

Adobe Photoshop

Adobe PageMaker

Materials:

Clipping path templates

Certificate templates

Your photo

Project 21

Creating Awards and Certificates

Create professional, attractive certificates and awards.

With Photoshop's clipping path feature, you can make your photo appear inside a specially shaped area, such as an oval. You can then place this shaped photo into a certificate template to create personalized award documents.

Clipping paths let you cut out unwanted areas around an object or portion of a photo. When you place a clipped image in another application, the shaped edges of the image display seamlessly against the background (see "Creating balanced border effects" on page 30).

① Getting started. In Photoshop, open your photo file. Then open a clipping path template in the Proj21 folder. Choose the template that matches the shape you want for your final photo.

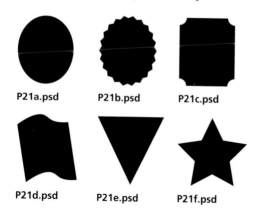

P21a.psd   P21b.psd   P21c.psd

P21d.psd   P21e.psd   P21f.psd

②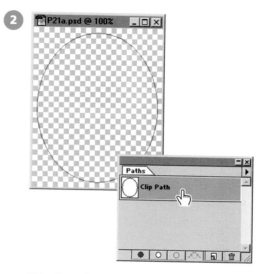

Display the template path. Make the template image window active. In the Paths palette, click to select the clipping path that appears in the list.

Selecting the path displays it in the image. Although the clipping path is currently visible, it will not print as part of the image. Instead, it will act as a "cookie cutter," shaping the content of your final photo.

3

Drag and drop your photo on the template. Select the move tool (▸⊹) and drag your photo to the clipping path template, releasing the mouse when the template window becomes highlighted. Close the photo file when you are finished.

Don't worry if only part of your photo is visible within the template boundaries. The parts outside the boundaries are still available, and can be brought into view in the next step.

4

Resize and reposition your photo. Choose Edit > Transform > Scale. Shift-drag a corner handle of the bounding box to resize the photo, and press Enter or Return. Drag the photo with the move tool (▸⊹) to bring a different part of the photo inside the clipping path.

5

Save working and export versions of the clipped photo. To save a layered working version, choose File > Save As, rename the file, and save it in Photoshop format. To save a single-layer version for export, choose File > Save a Copy, rename the file, and save it in TIFF format.

The TIFF format stores the clipping path information that you will need to place the photo properly.

6 **Open a certificate template.** In PageMaker, open a certificate template in the Awards folder inside the Proj21 folder.

P21a.t65

P21b.t65

P21c.t65

P21d.t65

P21e.t65

P21f.t65

P21g.t65

P21h.t65

7

Place the clipped photo in the certificate. Select the image frame in the template, and choose File > Place. Accept the current settings and place the TIFF version of the clipped photo. Click Yes to include the photo as part of the certificate file.

Notice that the clipping path creates a shaped image that fits nicely inside the premade frame.

8 **Enter your own certificate text.** Use the text tool (**T**) to replace the placeholder text with your own information.

When you have completed your certificate, choose File > Save As and save the file under a different name.

Variation: Select your own area to be clipped

Instead of using a premade clipping path template, you can define your own selection to use as a clipping path. By performing a few extra steps, you can achieve greater control over the shape of your image.

2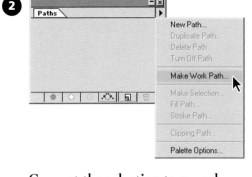

1

Select the area you want to keep.
With your photo file open and active in Photoshop, use any selection tool to select the area of the photo you want to retain. The clipping path will show only what's inside the selection, clipping out the areas outside the selection.

Convert the selection to a work path. Choose Make Work Path from the Paths palette menu. For Tolerance, enter **2.0**, and click OK. This converts your selection to a Photoshop path.

In the Paths palette, double-click the work path you just created. Name the path and click OK to save the work path as a permanent path.

3 **Define the clipping path.** Choose Clipping Path from the Paths palette menu. For Path, choose the path you just created, and click OK.

Variation: Draw your own path

Another variation involves drawing your path directly, rather than converting a selection. Drawing gives you enhanced control over the shape and smoothness of the path, allowing you to clip your image with greater precision. Remember that a clipping path can only be created from a path that forms a closed loop, such as a circle.

Draw or import a path. Create a path in one of the following ways:

• With your photo file open in Photoshop, draw a path using the freeform pen tool (✒), the magnetic pen tool (✒), or the pen tool (✒).

• In Illustrator or another vector drawing program, draw the desired shape outline. Select the shape and choose Edit > Copy. Switch to Photoshop, choose Edit > Paste, select Paste As Paths, and click OK.

② **Save the work path.** In Photoshop, double-click the work path in the Paths palette. Name the path and click OK to save the work path as a permanent path.

③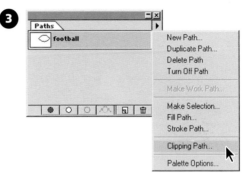

Define the clipping path. Choose Clipping Path from the Paths palette menu. For Path, choose the path you just created, and click OK.

④ **Resize and reposition your photo.** If needed, follow the instructions in step 4 of the project to resize and position the photo inside the clipping path.

DESIGN TIP: Using fonts in certificates

When choosing a font to use in your certificate, consider the theme and style of the award you are giving. Select fonts that reflect your award's special character.

When used wisely, script fonts lend a dignified, classical air to certificates. Try to avoid using script fonts in excess and in all capital letters.

Good certificate fonts provide clear, well-defined letter shapes suitable for display in large sizes. The following are some font suggestions from the Adobe Type Library, available from Adobe Systems:

Calligraphic

Caflisch Script® MM

Ex Ponto™ MM

Poetica® 1

Poetica 2 Supplement

Gothic

Goudy Text™

Notre Dame

Oxford™

San Marco

Classic-Roman

Caslon Open Face

Delphin I/Delphin II

University™ Roman

Modern

Bernhard Modern

Goudy Modern™

Adobe Jenson™ MM

Contemporary

ITC Isadora®

Park Avenue®

Present

Script

Bickham Script™ MM

Boulevard™

Shelley

Tools:

Adobe ImageReady

Materials:

Banner template

Your logo

Project 22

Creating an Animated Web Page Banner

Animate your logo and add a message to create a simple yet effective banner for your Web site.

Creating an animated banner using your company logo is an easy way to grab the attention of customers and establish corporate identity on a Web site. Here is a technique for making your logo move across a banner and a message gradually appear.

1 **Getting started.** In ImageReady, open the P22a.psd file (or one of the other banner templates in the Proj22 folder). The background area is 468 pixels by 60 pixels—the standard Web banner size.

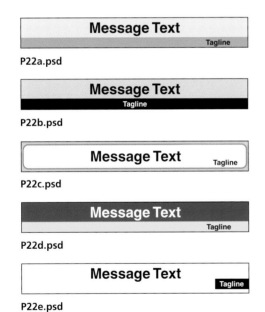

Message Text
Tagline

P22a.psd

Message Text
Tagline

P22b.psd

Message Text   Tagline

P22c.psd

Message Text
Tagline

P22d.psd

Message Text
Tagline

P22e.psd

2 Message Text
Tagline

Place your artwork. Choose File > Place Image, click Choose Image, and select your company logo. Place it within the borders of the banner. Repeat this step for other artwork you want to add to your banner.

Notice that in the Layers palette the image now has at least four layers—one for your logo, one called Message Text, one called Tagline, and a background layer. (Some of the templates have layers for more than one background color.) If you have imported other artwork, layers for that artwork also appear in the Layers palette.

③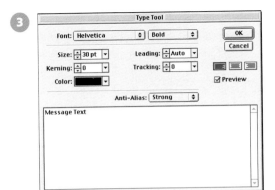

Customize the text. In the Layers palette, double-click the Message Text layer to edit it. In the Type Tool dialog box, select the text and replace it with your own. You can also change the font, size, and color. Click OK when you're done and then repeat this step to edit the text on the Tagline layer.

④

Arrange the layout for the animation. In the Layers palette, select the logo's layer and use the move tool (✛) to arrange the logo in the final position of the animation. Repeat this step to arrange all the artwork and text where you want it to finally appear in the banner.

⑤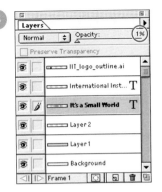

Create a fade-in effect. In the Layers palette, select each layer that you want to fade in (in this example, the message and tagline text layers) and set the opacity to 1% by dragging the Opacity slider all the way to the left. This is the starting opacity for the text fade.

⑥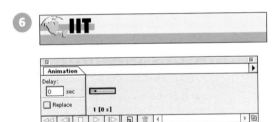

Create an animation. Show the Animation palette if it's not visible. You use this palette to add movement to your graphics and text. Notice that just one frame appears in the palette. This is the first frame of your animation.

7

Create an ending animation frame.
Click the New Frame button at the
bottom of the palette to create a new
frame. This will become the end frame
for the first part of the animation.

8

**Set the animation's starting
position.** In the Animation palette,
select the first frame. In the Layers
palette, select the logo layer. In the
image window, use the move tool to
reposition the logo all the way to the
right of the banner. This is the starting
position for the animated logo.

9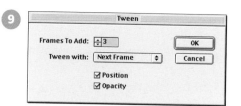

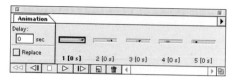

Tween the logo animation. In the
Animation palette, choose Tween from
the palette menu. Enter 3 for Frames to
Add and select Tween with Next
Frame. Make sure that Position and
Opacity are selected and click OK.
ImageReady adds frames to make the
logo move from right to left. Notice
that five frames now appear in the
Animation palette. You have just
created movement!

10 Complete the text fade. Select the last frame (frame 5) in the Animation palette. Click the New Frame button to create a new frame (frame 6) and then make sure that the new frame is selected. In the Layers palette, select the layer with the fade-in effect (in this example, the message text) and use the Opacity slider to set its Opacity to 100%. Repeat this step if you have more than one layer to fade. Now you'll make the text fade in as the logo moves across it.

12 Set the delay, repeat, and pause. To slow down the animation, choose Set Delay for All Frames from the Animation palette menu and enter a delay of **0.7** second.

To control how often the animation repeats, choose Play Options from the Animation palette menu. Select Forever for continuous play, Once for one loop, or enter the number of the repetitions.

To pause an individual frame, such as your text frame, select the frame, and then enter a value in the Delay text box.

11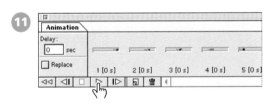

Tween the logo and text fade animation. With frame 6 selected, choose Tween from the Animation palette menu. Enter **3** for Frames to Add and select Tween with Previous Frame, Position, and Opacity. This creates the frames to change the opacity and fade in your message.

Click the Play button (▷) to view what you've set up. Then click the Stop button (□).

13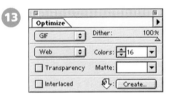

Optimize your image. In the Optimize palette, choose GIF from the file format pop-up menu (GIF is the only format that supports animation). Choose Web from the color palette menu or, if your banner includes photographs or artwork containing color gradients, choose the Adaptive color palette. For tips on reducing the file size, see "Optimizing image files for the Web" on page 151.

Preview the optimized image. At the top of the image window, click the Optimized tab to preview how the file will look when exported. A progress bar appears as ImageReady reduces the file size and image color for the Web while keeping the best possible quality.

 Save working and optimized versions of the image. Choose File > Save Original As, rename the file, and save a working version of the banner. This saves the file in Photoshop format and keeps all the layers intact.

Then choose File > Save Optimized, and save the file with a different name. ImageReady flattens the file to a single layer and compresses the image into GIF format. The animated GIF image is now ready to be added to your Web page.

When creating animations, consider that even a little motion makes a big impact. Make sure that your animation piece is not too distracting on the page and is easy to read. Graphics that flash too quickly or use bright, neon colors deter viewers rather than attract their attention. Try to make changes between frames subtle.

If you're using a photograph, make sure that it does not interfere with other elements on the page. Remember that animations must be saved in GIF format. Use the Perceptual or Adaptive color palette for better quality continuous-tone images.

Before you start to record the animation, place all of your image files and arrange all pieces of your design. If you try to reposition graphics after you've started to record, your design can quickly become confused.

Give your readers time to read the banner before starting the animation over. Either run the animation only once or insert a pause between loops.

You can set up animations using layered files created in either ImageReady or Photoshop. For more information, see Project 23, "Using Layers to Animate a Web Banner" on page 152. Alternatively, in Adobe Illustrator 8.0, you can draw graphics using Web-safe colors on a separate layer, and then export the file in Photoshop 5 format.

Keep the text simple and use clean, sans serif or bold fonts—such as those in a highway billboard.

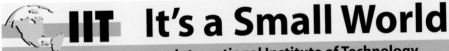

Use Web-safe colors to ensure consistent colors with no dithering. For more information, see Input/Output on the next page.

File size is an important consideration when preparing an image file for the Web. Keep it small. As a rule of thumb, 12K is a good size for banners. This size lets the page download quickly.

Previewing the image as you optimize it

As you select Optimize settings for your image, you can preview the effect in the image window. You can also choose View > Browser Dither to see a simulation of how a Web browser will dither image colors on an 8-bit system. Dithering simulates colors not available on display systems by adjusting adjacent pixels of different colors to give the appearance of a third color.

Optimizing flat-color or animated images

For flat-color images with few colors (such as logos and typefaces) or animated images, use the GIF format.

○ Choose the Web color palette to make your image look best in the standard 216 colors on all monitors and browsers.

○ In cases when you need to optimize photographs or images with gradients in GIF format, choose the Adaptive color palette to avoid color banding.

○ Click the Optimize tab in the image window to preview the image.

○ Check in the status bar at the bottom of the image window to see what the file size will be for the current settings.

○ Try using fewer colors by choosing a value from the Colors pop-up menu in the Optimize palette. Keep an eye on image quality and file size as you try different settings. To see the image's color table, show the Optimized Colors palette.

○ Drag the Dither slider in the Optimize palette and preview the image to lower the amount of dithering while maintaining the image quality. The less the dithering, the smaller the file.

Optimizing photographs

For photographs and continuous-tone images with subtle color gradations, use the JPEG format.

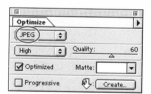

Drag the Quality slider to control the amount of compression. The higher the quality, the less the compression and the bigger the file.

Tools:

Adobe ImageReady

Adobe Photoshop

Materials:

Banner templates

Your photo

Project 23

Using Layers to Animate a Web Banner

Show or hide layers to make graphics move, ideas appear, and company slogans grow in your Web banner.

By turning on or off layers containing type, images, or graphics, you can easily create animated effects on your Web site. For even greater impact, you can combine photographic images from Photoshop with animations in ImageReady. When creating graphics for the Web, you should use 72 ppi images in RGB color mode. You can start with one of the ImageReady templates that contains several layers.

Getting started. In ImageReady, open the P23a.psd file (one of the layered banner templates in the Proj23 folder). The banner dimensions match the standard Web banner size of 468 pixels by 60 pixels.

Replace the template type. In the Layers palette, double-click the type layer to select it and display the Type

Tool dialog box. Select the type and replace it with your own slogan, changing the font and color if you like.

Crop and resize a photo. In Photoshop or other image-editing software, crop and resize your photo to fit the semicircular transparent area of the banner template. Your photo must be at least 119 pixels in diameter to fit the circular cutout. For tips on cropping and image resizing, see "Crop and refine the photo size" on page 6.

Add your photo. In ImageReady, open your photographic image. Use a selection tool to select part of the image or choose Select > All to select all of the image. Then use the move tool (⊕) to drag the selection and drop it on the template file. This creates a new layer for the selection. Scale the photo if needed by choosing Edit > Transform > Scale and dragging the handles. Use the move tool to position the photo in the lower left corner, in the area provided in the template.

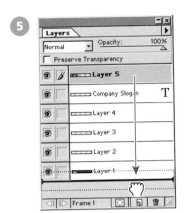

5

Arrange the layers. In the Layers palette, drag your photo layer to the bottom of the palette. The layer above has a cutout for the photo to show through. In the image window, use the move tool to position your photo if needed.

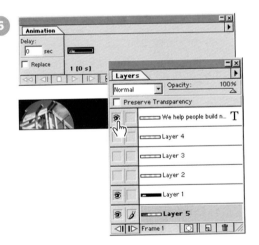

6

Set up the animation. In the Animation palette, a frame shows a thumbnail image of the banner. This is the first frame of your animation. In the Layers palette, click the eye icons to

hide Layers 2, 3, and 4 and your type layer, so that only the photo layer and Layer 1 are visible. You have just designed the first frame.

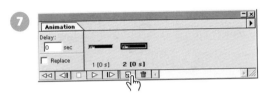

7

Create new frames. Click the New Frame button in the Animation palette (a new frame labeled 2 appears) and then click the leftmost column in the Layers palette next to Layer 2 to display the layer.

Repeat this step for Layers 3 and 4 and the type layer, to create new frames that show the layers.

Click the Play button (▷) to view what you've set up. Then click the Stop button (□).

8 **Set the delay, repeat, and pause.** To slow down the animation, choose Set Delay for All Frames from the Animation palette menu and enter a delay of **0.7** second.

To control how often the animation repeats, choose Play Options from the Animation palette menu. Select Forever for continuous play, Once for one loop, or enter the number of the repetitions.

To pause an individual frame, such as your slogan frame, select the frame, and then enter a value in the Delay text box.

10 **Save original and optimized versions of your image.** Choose File > Save Original As, rename the file, and save a working version of the animated banner. This saves the file in Photoshop format and keeps all the layers intact.

Then choose File > Save Optimized, and save the file with a different name. ImageReady flattens the file to a single layer and compresses the image into GIF format. The animated GIF image is now ready to be added to your Web page.

9

Optimize the banner image. In the Optimize palette, choose GIF from the file format pop-up menu and Adaptive from the color palette menu. GIF is the only format that supports animation. For tips on reducing the file size, see "Optimizing image files for the Web" on page 151.

Variation: Customize additional templates

Other banner templates in the Proj23 folder contain multiple type layers and different graphics that you can customize.

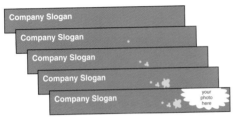

P23b.psd—Make your photo gradually appear.

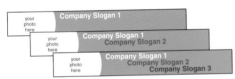

P23c.psd—Build your slogan line by line.

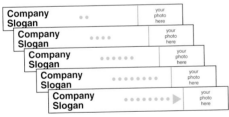

P23d.psd—Animate the dotted arrow.

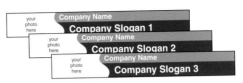

P23e.psd—Change the slogan in each frame.

P23f.psd—Make the ribbon ripple in the wind.

1 **Customize a banner template with multiple type layers.** Follow steps 2 through 4 in the project and customize the banner with your own type and photo.

2 **Customize the animation order.** In step 6, choose any combination of layers to show in the first frame. (The layers do not have to be in order). In step 7, click the New Frame button and select the layers you want to show; then repeat these steps to create as many frames as desired. Keep in mind that the file size increases with more frames.

3

Customize graphic colors. Select a graphic layer and frame in the Animation palette and use the magic wand tool (✳) to select a color in the graphic. Then use the Color palette or the Color Picker to choose a new foreground color and press Alt+Backspace (Windows) or Option+Delete (Mac OS) to fill the selected area.

For Photoshop techniques on coloring photographic images, see "Coloring Photographs by Hand" on page 18.

4 **Use ImageReady actions.** Choose from the actions supplied in ImageReady to create drop shadows and textures. Then add them to your banner.

For design tips and more techniques for animating your banner, see "Creating an Animated Web Page Banner" on page 144.

Tools:

Adobe ImageReady

Materials:

Navigation bar templates

Your logo

Project 24

Creating a Navigation Bar for the Web

Create a navigation bar to link major locations in your site.

A navigation bar helps Web site visitors find information quickly and stay oriented in your site. You can use a navigation bar on every page in a site, or create multiple navigation bars and highlight a button to indicate the reader's location.

To create a horizontal or vertical navigation bar, customize an ImageReady template and link its buttons and icons to your Web pages. Then save an optimized version of the navigation bar along with an HTML page that you can open in your Web page design program.

P24a.psd

P24b.psd

P24c.psd

P24d.psd

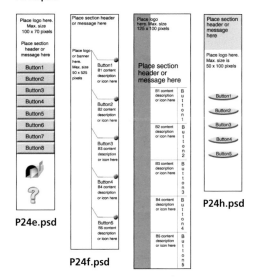

P24e.psd

P24f.psd

P24g.psd

P24h.psd

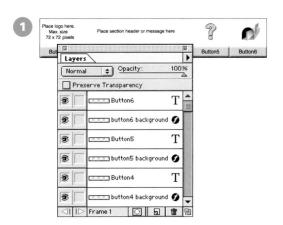

Getting started. In ImageReady, open the P24a.psd file (or choose one of the other templates for horizontal and vertical navigation bars in the Proj24 folder).

In the Layers palette, notice that the template has several layers. You'll see in a moment how working with layers makes editing the template quick and easy.

2

Place your logo. Choose File > Place Image and then click Choose Image and select your logo file or other art file that you want to place in the Navigation bar. In the Layers palette, click the eye icon for the Place Your Logo layer to hide the layer.

3 **Add your company message.** In the Layers palette, double-click the Place Section Header Or Message Here layer. In the Type Tool dialog box, select the existing text and replace it with your company name or a message. You can see the message text in the navigation bar as you type it. If necessary, select the new text and change the font size. You can also change the font or color.

If you don't want to add your company name or a message here, click the layer's eye icon to hide the layer.

4

Type your button text. In the Layers palette, double-click the Button1 layer. Select the existing text and replace it with your button text. Adjust the size, font, and color of the text as needed.

Type and format the text for the remaining buttons in the same way.

5

Change the background colors. You can change the background colors of the navigation bar and the buttons. In the Layers palette, select the navigation bar's background layer. (In some templates there are two background layers for gray and white areas.) Select a color in the Color palette and then click in the background area of the image with the paint bucket tool ().

If the template you are using has separate button backgrounds, select the button's background layer and then select a color and apply it with the paint bucket tool.

To ensure consistency and no dithering, use Web-safe colors.

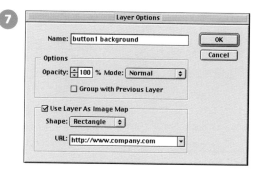

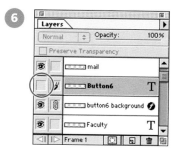

Remove unused buttons. In the Layers palette, click to hide the eye icon for any unused button's text and background layers. The button text is linked to its background layer, so you can easily rearrange the remaining buttons in the navigation bar. If you want to resize the buttons using the Transform commands, unlink the button background from the text so it won't distort the text.

Some of the templates include a question mark icon and mailbox icon. Hide these layers if you don't want to use them.

Link the buttons to your Web pages. In the Layers palette, double-click a button background layer. Select Use Layer as Image Map, and then enter the path to the Web page that you are linking to.

Use a relative path for pages in your Web site. For example, if you keep all your Web pages and image files in a single folder, the path would consist of the filename of the page.

You can also link to a page that's not on your site. If you do, make sure you enter the complete URL, for example, http://www.adobe.com.

Repeat this step for the remaining button backgrounds, and for the mailbox and question mark icons if you are using them.

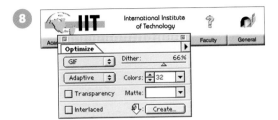

8

Optimize your image. In the Optimize palette, choose GIF from the file format pop-up menu and Adaptive from the color palette pop-up menu. For tips on reducing the file size, see "Optimizing image files for the Web" on page 151.

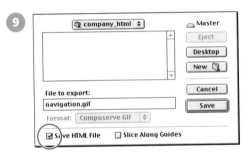

9

Save original and optimized versions of the image. Choose File > Save Original As, rename the file, and save a working version of the navigation bar. This saves the file in Photoshop format and keeps all the layers intact.

Then choose File > Save Optimized, select Save HTML File, and save the file with a different name. ImageReady saves two files—a compressed image file with the .gif extension and a Web page with the .html extension.

10 **Edit the Web page.** In your Web page design application, open the HTML file you just created. You can continue adding content to this page or you can copy the source code from the page and paste it into your own pages. For information on copying the code, see "Using the navigation bar in your Web pages" on page 165.

Variation: Create highlighted buttons

You've probably seen navigation bars that show where you are in a Web site. Here is a technique to highlight the text of navigation buttons. You'll need to save several versions of the navigation bar—one for each highlighted button. The navigation bar with a different highlighted button will appear on each Web page, depending on which button is linked to the page.

1 **Duplicate the button text layers.** For each button text layer, drag the layer to the new layer icon in the Layers palette. With the new layer selected, choose Layer Options from the pop-up menu and add "highlight" to the layer's name.

②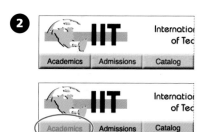

Change the text color of the dupli-cates. In the Layers palette, double-click a duplicate button text layer and choose a highlight color from the Color pop-up menu. Repeat this step for each of the duplicate text layers.

Now you have two versions of each button text layer — one with the original color and one with the highlight color.

③ Set the visible layers for the first button. For the first button, click the eye icon to hide the original button text layer and make sure the eye icon is showing for the highlighted text layer. The remaining buttons should have the original text showing and the highlighted text hidden.

④ Export the first navigation bar. Choose File > Save Optimized As, select Save HTML File, and save the navigation bar with a different name.

⑤ Set visible layers and export the remaining navigation bars. Repeat steps 3 and 4 for each highlighted button. You'll end up with a new Web page for each highlighted button.

When you begin designing a navigational system, you will want to have a clear idea of where it needs to take your readers. Create a flowchart of your site to clearly map each location and how it can be accessed. It's a good idea to have all the main links accessible from the interior pages.

Map your site so you know its navigation needs.

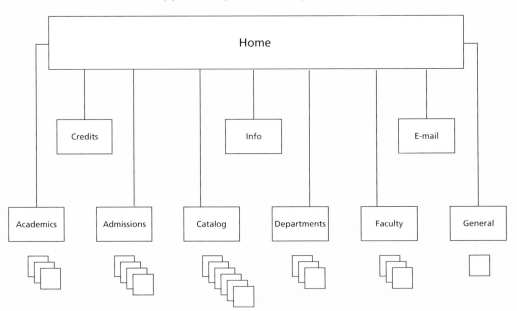

Copying the HTML code

To use the navigation bar in your own Web pages, you'll need to copy the HTML source code that ImageReady generated.

In your Web page design application, open the HTML file that ImageReady created. Switch to the source view and copy the HTML code for the image map and the navigation bar graphic. Make sure that you copy the text between the <Map ...> and </Map> tags and the text within the <IMG SRC ...> tag (including the tags).

Paste the code into the Body section of your Web page (right after the <Body> tag).

Slicing the navigation bar

If you are using multiple navigation bars with highlighted buttons to indicate your reader's location in a site, you might want to try this technique to save download times. Slice the navigation bar into two parts. One part contains the common elements of the navigation bars. The second part contains the buttons— including a highlighted button. Every Web page uses the same image for the common elements of the navigation bar. Since the image will be stored in the Web browser's cache, it doesn't need to be downloaded with each page your reader views.

The top part stays in the Web browser's cache. The bottom part is downloaded for each button that's clicked.

In ImageReady, you can set guides where you want the image to be sliced. The horizontal templates in the Proj24 folder have guides set to slice the navigation bar. To see the guides, choose View > Show Guides.

When you save the optimized navigation bar, make sure you select Slice Along Guides in the Save Optimized dialog box. ImageReady slices the navigation bar into two images and reassembles it by using an HTML table.

Use the Web page that ImageReady generates or copy the code into your pages. Make sure you copy all the code between the <Table ...> and the </Table> tags (including the tags).

Tools:

Adobe Photoshop

Adobe ImageReady

Materials:

Photoshop actions

Your photo

Project 25

Creating a Large Background for Your Web Page

Use your photo and a custom action to make a large background tile for pages on your Web site.

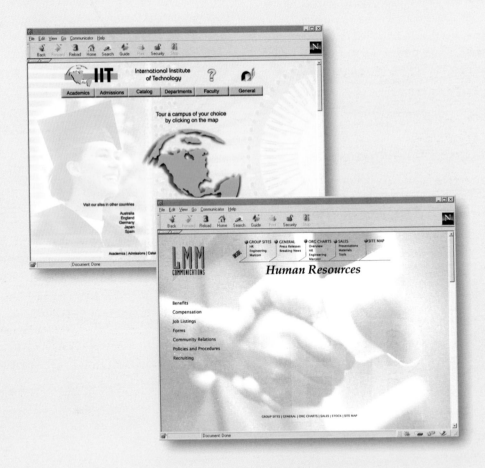

Normally, using a full-color photo large enough to fill the entire background of a Web page would result in a file that's too large for Web viewing. Here's a technique for creating an attractive monochromatic background image with a file size that is small enough to use as a background tile on your Web pages and yet large enough to fill the screen.

Getting started. In Photoshop, open your color photo and resize or crop it as necessary. In order for the image tile to fill the entire background of the Web page, the image should be 600 to 800 pixels wide and at least 480 pixels high. Choose an image size based on the amount of material on the page and how far you want your readers to scroll down before they see the next repeating tile.

For information on resizing images, see "Crop and refine the photo size" on page 6.

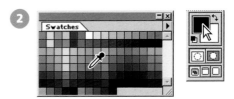

Select a color for the image. Click a color in the Swatches palette to select a foreground color, or click the Foreground Color box in the toolbox and select a color from the Color Picker.

Play a custom action. In the Actions palette, choose Load Actions from the pop-up menu and load the P25.atn file in the Proj25 folder. The P25.atn action set appears in the Actions palette. In the action set, select either the Colorize/Filmgrain, Colorize, or Wind action, and click the Play button on the palette.

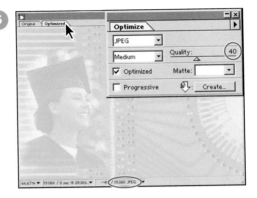

Adjust the color intensity. In the Layers palette, select the layer containing the foreground color and use the Opacity slider at the top of the palette to decrease the opacity of the color fill. This affects how much of the grayscale image shows through.

Save a working version of the image. Choose File > Save As and save the file in Photoshop format. Although you can save your image file in JPEG format in Photoshop, ImageReady gives you better compression control over your file.

Save and optimize the image in JPEG format. In ImageReady, open the image file. In the Optimize palette, choose JPEG from the pop-up menu, and drag the Quality slider to 40 or lower. (Keep the file size down to around 20K or lower, if possible.) For information on optimizing, see "Optimizing image files for the Web" on page 151.

Choose File > Save Optimized and save the file with a different name. ImageReady flattens the layers into a single layer and compresses the image into JPEG format. The JPEG image is now ready to be tiled in your Web page background.

Variation: Actions for different effects

Try out some of the other actions for different textured effects and to change the image to grayscale. These actions do not require a foreground color selection: Grayscale/Water Paper, Halftone/Extreme, and Grayscale/Halftone/Extreme.

DESIGN TIP: Using a large image for a Web page background

Incorporate graphic elements into your background image that will complement the other graphics in your page. This will give your Web page a more dynamic look. Limit the contents of your Web page to the length of the first tile to ensure that your readers don't scroll to the next repeating tile.

Make sure that the elements in your background do not interfere with the text on your page.

Two colors are all you need. Fewer colors will help keep the file size down.

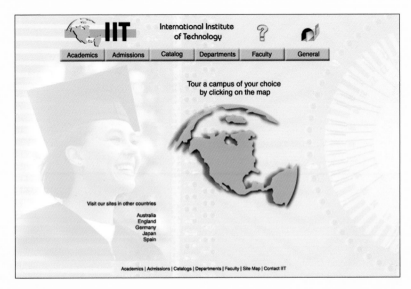

Use graphics that work with or complement the other graphics referenced by your Web page. Exact alignment is not necessary, as the placement of your other elements may vary a few pixels from browser to browser.

Dark, saturated background colors decrease the legibility of text.

Soft, neutral background colors help support a good Web design.

Tools:

Adobe Photoshop

Adobe ImageReady

Materials:

Texture files

Your photo

Project 26

Creating Buttons for the Web

Use your photo or a texture file to create a button for your Web page and save it in two on/off states.

Here's a technique for using a photo as the background texture of a button on your Web page. You'll create the button, add text, and then compress it as a GIF image. You can also create two on/off states for the button using Photoshop layer effects.

P26i.psd

P26j.psd

P26k.psd

P26l.psd

1 **Getting started.** In ImageReady, open your photo or one of several Photoshop sample files in the Proj26 folder to use for the texture of the button. Resize or crop the image to the desired button size. For information on image resizing, see "Crop and refine the photo size" on page 6.

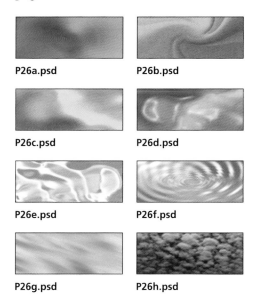

P26a.psd

P26b.psd

P26c.psd

P26d.psd

P26e.psd

P26f.psd

P26g.psd

P26h.psd

2

Create the button's edges. In the Actions palette, select and play one of these actions: Inner Bevel, Inner Shadow, or Sunken Bevel.

3

Add text. Select the type tool (T) and click in the image area of the button. In the Type Tool dialog box, type the text for the button. To preview how the new text will fit in the button, make sure that Preview is selected and that you can see the image of the button. Then select the text in the Type Tool dialog box and select a font and size.

4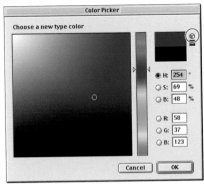

Change the text color. If you want to change the text color, click the Color box in the Type Tool dialog box and then choose a color from the Color Picker. If the cube icon appears next to your color choice, click it to shift the color to the closest Web-safe color. This will prevent your text from dithering when viewed on a monitor that can only display 256 colors. When you're done, click OK.

5 Español

Español

Reposition the text. If necessary, select the move tool (✛) and reposition the text or use the arrow keys to nudge the text in 1-pixel increments.

6 Optimize your image. In the Optimize palette, choose GIF from the file format pop-up menu and Adaptive from the color palette pop-up menu.

For tips on reducing the file size, see "Optimizing image files for the Web" on page 151.

7 Save original and optimized versions of the image. Choose File > Save Original As, rename the file, and save a working version of the button. This saves the file in Photoshop format and leaves all of the layers intact.

Then choose File > Save Optimized and save the file with a different name. ImageReady flattens the file to a single layer and compresses the image into GIF format. The GIF image is now ready to be added to your Web page.

For design tips and information on using buttons in a navigation bar, see Project 24, "Creating a Navigation Bar for the Web" on page 158.

Variation: Create on/off buttons

Apply an ImageReady action to your button to create two states for Java-script rollovers, where one of the states shows the button depressed when a reader clicks or moves the pointer over the button. With this technique, you don't need to create the button edges as you did in step 2 earlier. Just add text and change the color if you want.

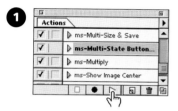

Play the action. In the Layers palette, select the background texture layer of the button. In the Actions palette, select the ms-Multi-State Button Maker action, click the Play button at the bottom of the palette, and then click Continue.

Save the changes. Choose File > Save Original and save the file.

You now have two background layers: one with the Inner Bevel effect applied to the button and one with the Sunken Bevel effect. Both layers also have the Inner Shadow effect.

Save the two button states. In the Layers palette, click the eye icon to hide one of the background texture layers, choose File > Save Optimized, and save the first button state. Then hide the other background texture layer and show the first one. Choose File > Save Optimized As and save the second button state with a different name.

Use the multistate button files in your Javascript or Web authoring program to create rollovers on your Web page.

Variation: Customize layer effect settings

Use Photoshop to change or apply additional effects to the layers of the button.

1 **Open the file.** In Photoshop, open the original version of the button file with all the layers intact (not the optimized GIF file).

2

Experiment with the layer effects. In the Layers palette, double-click the layer effects icon (⨀) on a layer to open the Effects dialog box. Select Preview and experiment with the settings for the applied effect, or deselect Apply and choose a different effect from the pop-up menu.

If you wish to apply the same effects to another layer, choose Layer > Effects > Copy Effects, select the other layer, and choose Layer > Effects > Paste Effects.

3 **Save the customized file.** In Adobe Photoshop, save the changes to the file. In ImageReady, reopen the file. (If the file was still open in ImageReady, click Yes to update the file.) Choose File > Save Optimized and save the changes in compressed GIF format.

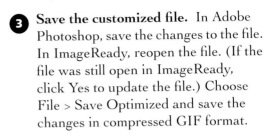

Use a bold sans serif font for the text on your buttons so it's easier to read on-screen.

Color-code your buttons to make navigation through your Web site easier.

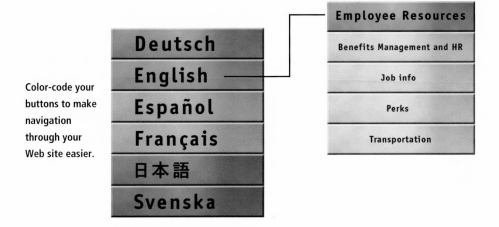

Bold-faced fonts with contrasting color increase legibility.

Light or serif fonts with minimal contrast are more difficult to read.

Use simple photos or textures that don't conflict with the text or icon on the button.

If you use a photograph, make sure that important parts of the photo are not right along the edges of the button where they'll be covered by the edge effect.

Appendix: Choosing a File Format

File formats encode the information in an image file so that the image can be used by another application or output device. Most projects instruct you to save two versions of your file—a working version in native Adobe Photoshop format, and an export or optimized version in a different format.

The Photoshop format retains full layer information, making it convenient for you to edit the file in the future. The export and optimized formats automatically flatten the file's visible layers into a single layer for transfer to other destinations.

Saving files for use in Photoshop and ImageReady

Both Photoshop and Adobe ImageReady have the ability to open files saved in a variety of formats. Nevertheless, you may occasionally encounter a file format that's difficult to open. If this happens, return to the application used to create or capture the file, and save the file in one of the following formats: TIFF, EPS, BMP (Windows), or PICT (Mac OS). Then open the file in Photoshop or ImageReady.

Saving files for export from Photoshop

The projects in this book recommend specific formats to use when exporting files from Photoshop to applications such as Adobe PageMaker or Adobe Illustrator. If you plan to export to another application, refer to that application's documentation for the appropriate format to use.

The TIFF, EPS, BMP (Windows), and PICT (Mac OS) formats are commonly supported by many applications. Keep in mind that you must use a PostScript printer to print EPS files correctly.

Choosing a Web format

Photoshop and ImageReady let you save files in several common formats supported on the World Wide Web. Each format uses a compression technique to reduce the file size and download time of the image file. When choosing a Web format, consider the color range and background transparency needs of the final image.

GIF The GIF format is effective at compressing solid-color images and images with areas of repetitive color such as line art, logos, or illustrations with type. This format uses a palette of up to 256 colors to represent the image, and supports background transparency. (See "Preserving transparency in an image" on page 31.)

JPEG The JPEG format is designed to preserve the broad color range and subtle brightness variations of continuous-tone images such as photographs or images with gradients. This format uses millions of colors to represent images.

PNG The PNG format is effective at compressing solid-color images and provides sophisticated transparency support. However, many older browser applications do not support PNG. ImageReady offers two versions of PNG: PNG-8 uses a 256-color palette to represent an image, while PNG-24 supports 24-bit color (millions of colors). (See "Preserving transparency in an image" on page 31.)

Index

Production Notes

This book was created electronically using Adobe FrameMaker®. Art was produced using Adobe Illustrator, Adobe ImageReady, Adobe Photoshop, and Adobe PageMaker. The Cochin and Frutiger families of typefaces are used throughout this book.

Photography Credits

Photographic images intended for use as samples only.

EyeWire, Inc.
Getting Photos Ready (*boy, business man, young woman, skier, person with kayak, young couple, cyclist, skater*); Project 3 (*clock*); Project 4 (*business man and woman, surfer*); Project 5 (*business woman, surfer*); Project 6 (*calculator, woman on phone*); Project 7 (*farm fields, microscope, windmills, violinist*); Project 12 (*woman's face*); Project 13 (*office supplies*); Project 14 (*all photos*); Project 15 (*bill, clock, abstract textures*); Project 17 (*all photos*); Project 18 (*CD*); Project 19 (*exercise woman, aerobics*); Project 20 (*background textures*); Project 22 (*skiers*); Project 23 (*house construction, compass, combination lock, chess*); Project 25 (*globe, hands*)

Adobe Studio
Project 1 (*posing man in suit*)

Benjamin Hollin
Getting Photos Ready (*woman on phone*); Project 18 (*CD*)

CMCD, Inc.
Project 21 (*gavel*)

Dean Dapkus
Project 7 (*child*)

Elizabeth Pham
Project 19 (*wedding photo*)

Julieanne Kost
Project 1 (*sky background*); Project 2 (*couch, chair, pumpkins*); Project 3 (*sand dune*); Project 9 (*all photos*); Project 11 (*watermelon, computer screen, toothbrushes, teapot*); Project 12 (*pliers, Golden Gate Bridge*); Project 15 (*sail boat, sunset, horses*); Project 16 (*all photos*); Project 26 (*plate*)

Kim Brown
Project 21 (*dog*)

Lisa Milosevich
Project 13 (*pens, scissors, notes*)

Photodisc, Inc.
Project 2 (*windmill*); Project 6 (*test tubes, dam, wheat*); Project 21 (*employee-of-the-year, football player*)

Susan Horovitz
Project 10 (*house*)

Adobe Typefaces Used

Project 2: Impact, *pkg. 211*; Post-Antiqua, *pkg. 092*

Project 3: Frutiger, *pkg. 073*; Adobe Garamond Expert, *pkg. 101*

Project 4: ITC Esprit, *pkg. 267*; Frutiger, *pkg. 073*

Project 5: ITC Century Handtooled, *pkg. 379*; ITC Esprit, *pkg. 267*; Frutiger, *pkg. 073*; Gills Sans, *pkg. 162*; Snell Roundhand, *pkg. 147*

Project 6: Frutiger, *pkg. 073*; Lucida Sans, *pkg. 048*; Strayhorn MT, *pkg. 452*

Project 7: Caflisch Script MM, *pkg. 359*; Frutiger, *pkg. 073*; Minion, *pkg. 143*; Nueva MM, *pkg. 378*

Project 8: Minion, *pkg. 143*; Myriad MM, *pkg. 275*; Poetica 1, *pkg. 300*; Poetica 2, *pkg. 301*; Waters Titling® MM, *pkg. 442*

Project 9: Frutiger Condensed, *pkg. 261*; Linoscript, *pkg. 094*

Project 11: Berliner Grotesk, *pkg. 311*; Caliban, *pkg. 388*; Clairvaux, *pkg. 229*; Immi 505, *pkg. 445*

Project 13: Bossa Nova MVB, *pkg. 447*; Caslon 3, *pkg. 053*; Granjon, *pkg. 205*

Project 14: Bossa Nova MVB, *pkg. 447*; Granjon, *pkg. 205*

Project 15: Adobe Garamond, *pkg. 100*; Flyer Black, *pkg. 149*; Frutiger, *pkg. 073*; Ocean Sans MM, *pkg. 405*

Project 17: Delphin II, *pkg. 387*, Koch-Antiqua, p*kg. 387*; Univers Extra Black & Ultra Condensed, *pkg. 191*

Project 18: Frutiger, *pkg. 073*; Lucida Sans, *pkg. 048*; Optima 1, *pkg. 006*

Project 19: Frutiger, *pkg. 073*; Frutiger Condensed, *pkg. 261*; Futura 2, *pkg. 046*; Memphis, *pkg. 049*

Project 20: ITC Esprit, *pkg. 267*; ITC Franklin Gothic, *pkg. 023*; Gills Sans 2, *pkg. 162*; Snell Roundhand, *pkg. 147*

Project 21: ITC Berkeley Old Style, *pkg. 106*; Bernhard Modern, *pkg. 352*; Bickham Script MM, *pkg. 435*; Boulevard, *pkg. 260*; Caslon 3 SC+OsF, *pkg. 241*; Caslon Open Face, *pkg. 072*; Caflisch Script MM, *pkg. 359*; ITC Century Handtooled, *pkg. 379*; Delphin I/Delphin II, *pkg. 387*; El Greco, *pkg. 395*; Ex Ponto MM, *pkg. 385*; Goudy Modern, *pkg. 305*; Goudy Text, *pkg. 242*; ITC Isadora, *pkg. 285*; Adobe Jenson MM, *pkg. 400*; Minion, *pkg. 143*; Notre Dame, *pkg. 372*; Nueva MM, *pkg. 378*; Oxford, *pkg. 339*; Park Avenue, *pkg. 025*; Poetica 1, *pkg. 300*; Poetica 2, *pkg. 301*; Present, *pkg. 271*; San Marco, *pkg. 229*; Shelley, *pkg. 136*; University Roman, *pkg. 034*

Project 22: ITC Bauhaus, *pkg. 087*; Frutiger, *pkg. 073*; Lithos, *pkg. 121*; Myriad MM, *pkg. 275*; Old Claude LP, *pkg. 436*

Project 23: Frutiger, *pkg. 073*; Strayhorn MT, *pkg. 452*; Strayhorn MT SC+OsF, *pkg. 453*

Project 24: ITC Bauhaus, *pkg. 087*; Industria, *pkg. 116*; Lucida Sans, *pkg. 048*

Project 25: Industria, *pkg. 116*; Lucida Sans, *pkg. 048*

Project 26: Frutiger, *pkg. 073*; Frutiger Condensed, *pkg. 261*; ITC Officina Sans, *pkg. 357*